Michael Rukavina

July 30, 1974

# *Problems of Mind*

*the text of this book is printed
on 100% recycled paper*

# HARPER ESSAYS IN PHILOSOPHY
*Edited by Arthur Danto*

---

| | |
|---|---|
| Arthur Danto | WHAT PHILOSOPHY IS |
| Norwood Russell Hanson | EXPLANATION AND OBSERVATION: A GUIDE TO PHILOSOPHY OF SCIENCE |
| Jerrold Katz | UNDERLYING REALITY OF LANGUAGE AND ITS PHILOSOPHICAL IMPORT |
| Norman Malcolm | PROBLEMS OF MIND |
| David Pears | WHAT IS KNOWLEDGE? |
| Hilary Putnam | PHILOSOPHY OF LOGIC |
| B. A. O. Williams | ETHICS |
| Robert Paul Wolff | IN DEFENSE OF ANARCHISM |
| Richard Wollheim | ART AND ITS OBJECTS |

# Problems of Mind

## Descartes to Wittgenstein

—————◆◆◆—————

## Norman Malcolm

**HARPER TORCHBOOKS**
Harper & Row, Publishers
New York, Evanston, San Francisco, London

# *Contents*

# *Preface*

———◆◆◆———

This essay was originally planned as one in a volume of essays by several authors. It was completed and delivered in September 1965. During subsequent years, while it languished in the hands of the publisher, there appeared a number of works that treat some of the topics discussed in this essay. I regret that it contains no reference to them.

Part I (Mind and Body) begins with a consideration of the view that the human mind is an immaterial thing that does not require corporeal embodiment for its operations. The assumptions that nourish this conception are studied, and some of the typical turns and twists of objection and reply are traced out. My conclusion is that the undermining, by Wittgenstein, of the notion that we obtain our psychological concepts (thinking, perception, memory, belief, will and so on) by "inward observation" (Locke's "inner sense"), removes the main temptation to believe that a human mind could exist in separation from a living, corporeal, human being.

Part II (Materialism) takes up the conception that
"inner experiences" are, or might turn out to be,
"strictly identical" with brain processes. I concentrate on the presentation of this view by J. J. C.
Smart, according to whom our "immediate" or
"inner" experiences take place "inside our skulls"
(*Journal of Philosophy* 60, 1963, p. 654) or "in our
brains" (*Philosophy and Scientific Realism,* p. 96).
Against the possibility of an empirical verification
of the claimed identity of an "inner experience"
with a correlated brain process, I urge what has
been called "the location problem." To a previous
presentation of this criticism, it has been objected
that a mind-brain materialist could contend that the
putative identity holds between the event that consists in a person's having a certain experience and
the event that consists in his brain's being in a certain state. Since neither of these events has location
in any clear sense, the location *disparity* is removed.
(See Jaegwon Kim, "On the Psycho-Physical Identity Theory," *American Philosophical Quarterly*
3, 1966, pp. 227–35.) It is true that someone could
adopt this view; and this shows that "the psycho-
physical identity theory" is not *one* theory, but a
collection of different theories or possible theories.
I have used the location argument solely against
Smart's version of identity theory, to which it re-
mains a decisive objection. With regard to the different theory just mentioned, I should think two
things: first, that it is more *artificial* than Smart's
theory, in the sense that it fails to embody the strong

temptation to think of experiences and mental phenomena as "inner." This temptation is a motive
force behind Smart's theory and is, I believe, the
main source of its philosophical interest. Second, as
Kim points out (*supra*), this suggested version of
identity theory, for which location is not a problem,
would be faced with the equally severe difficulty of
explaining how it could be verified that the *property*
of, say, having an orange after-image, is (or is not)
contingently identical (that is, not logically equivalent and not merely coextensive) with the *property*
of having a certain brain-state. The notion that these
two properties might turn out to be one and the same
property, despite their not being logically equivalent, would seem to be as meaningless as is the
notion, in Smart's theory, of verifying that an experience and a brain process have the same location
inside the skull.

In a recent book (*A Materialist Theory of the
Mind*, New York: Humanities Press, 1968) David
Armstrong argues in support of psycho-physical
identity theory by claiming (1) that the concept of
a mental state is the concept of an "inner cause" of
"outward behavior"; (2) that the inner cause of this
behavior is in fact a brain state; (3) that, therefore,
mental states *are* brain states. Unfortunately, I do
not have the space in this preface to explore these
contentions.

If I were writing Part II again, I should fix my
attention on the assumption called "The Principle
of Psycho-Physical Correspondence" or "The Prin-

ciple of Simultaneous Isomorphism.'' It has been assumed almost universally by philosophers and psychologists that a particular memory (or desire, or thought, or sensation) could be "isomorphic" with a particular state of the brain. As Wolfgang Köhler puts it, "cortical correlates of experience are isomorphic with this experience itself.'' Nowadays this is frequently stated as the notion that thoughts, ideas, memories, sensations, and so on, "code into" or "map onto" neural firing patterns in the brain. I believe that a study of our psychological concepts can show that psycho-physical isomorphism is not a coherent assumption.

Part III deals exclusively with the doctrine called "Logical Behaviorism." Although this position does not have the vogue it enjoyed in the 1930s and 1940s, it will always possess a compelling attraction for anyone who is perplexed by the psychological concepts, who has become aware of the worthlessness of an appeal to introspection as an account of how we learn those concepts, and who has no inclination to identify mind with brain.

There are other forms of behaviorism, and of reductionism, which I might have discussed in this essay if space had allowed. If I were writing it now I should pay attention to the controversy in psychology between "peripheral" and "central" theories of behavior. I should take particular note of the theories of "cognitive psychology" and of linguistics that attempt to explain behavioral and linguistic skills in terms of "central" processes or structures, variously called "cognitive maps," "schemata," "strategies," "systems of rules," "plans," or "abstract representations." Such a study would naturally lead to an examination of the currently popular view that a knowledge of computing machines and programs will increase our understanding of human thinking, memory and rational behavior.

A reader of this essay may feel that the outcome is too negative. The three most plausible theories (mind-body dualism, mind-brain monism, behaviorism) are all rejected, and nothing is set forth as the true theory. I readily admit that this essay is only a drop in the bucket. It will serve its purpose if it leads the reader into the writings of Wittgenstein, who is easily the most important figure in the philosophy of mind.[1] It should not be expected, however, that the reflections and observations of his *Philosophical Investigations* or his *Zettel* will somehow add up to another theory. To use his metaphor, philosophical work of the right sort merely unties knots in our understanding. The result is not a theory but simply—no knots!

Norman Malcolm
July 1970

1. In a recent article I have attempted to increase the "availability" of Wittgenstein's thinking on problems of mind. See my "Wittgenstein on the Nature of Mind," *American Philosophical Quarterly, Monograph* No. 4, N. Rescher, ed., Oxford, 1970.

# Problems of Mind

# I.
# Mind and Body

———◆◇◆———

## 1. A Mysterious Union

Descartes created a picture of the relationship between the human mind and the human body with
which philosophy has struggled ever since. The problem of the nature of mind is a region which, perhaps
more than any other, reveals the weakness, the per-
plexities and, sometimes, the power of human
thought. The variety and depth of confusion dis-
played there can astonish and dismay us. When we
trace the history of it we are, in the words of Thomas
Reid, "led into a labyrinth of fanciful opinions, con-
tradictions, and absurdities, intermixed with some
truths."[1]

The relation of mind to body has been commonly
felt by philosophers to be acutely difficult and even
incomprehensible. Hume summarized this feeling in
his rhetorical question:

---

1. Thomas Reid, *Works*, ed. W. Hamilton, 5th ed. (Edinburgh,
1858), *Essays on the Intellectual Powers*, Essay I, Ch. 5.

Is there any principle in all nature more mysterious than the union of soul with body; by which a supposed spiritual substance acquires such an influence over a material one, that the most refined thought is able to actuate the grossest matter? Were we empowered, by a secret wish, to remove mountains, or control the planets in their orbit, this extensive authority would not be more extraordinary, nor more beyond our comprehension.[2]

William James remarked that

mental and physical events are, on all hands, admitted to present the strongest contrast in the entire field of being. The chasm which yawns between them is less easily bridged over by the mind than any interval we know.[3]

## 2. Cartesian Dualism

In order to establish certainty in metaphysics in the place of error and conjecture, Descartes undertook to "reject as absolutely false" everything in regard to which he "could imagine the least ground of doubt."[4] This procedure would seem to consist in asserting the negation of any proposition the truth of which is subject to any possible ground of doubt. A general ground of doubt that struck at many of

2. David Hume, *Enquiry Concerning the Human Understanding,* ed. L. A. Selby-Bigge, 2nd ed. (Oxford, 1902), Sec. 7, Part 1.

3. William James, *The Principles of Psychology* (New York, 1890), Vol. 1, p. 134.

4. René Descartes, *Philosophical Works,* ed. E. Haldane and G. Ross (New York, 1955), Vol. 1, p. 101; *Discourse on the Method,* Part IV.

his former "opinions" was the possibility of his being so constituted that *none* of his perceptions corresponded to reality. Even his belief that he is placed in a material universe and *a fortiori,* his belief that he has a body, might be false. He can reject these beliefs without falling into any apparent absurdity. But matters stand differently when it comes to doubting his own existence. If he has this doubt he must exist. This doubt is, therefore, absurd. He cannot even conceive that he does not exist, although he still can conceive that he has no body. "I saw that I could conceive that I had no body, and that there was no world nor place where I might be; but yet that I could not for all that conceive that I was not."[5]

Descartes wishes to discover the nature of this "I" that he knows to exist. He comes to the conclusion that his nature or essence is solely *thinking.* "What then am I? A thing which thinks. What is a thing which thinks? It is a thing which doubts, understands, conceives, affirms, denies, wills, refuses, which also imagines and feels."[6]

In holding that he was solely a thinking thing Descartes excluded body from his essential nature. What considerations led him to this result? One simple argument he uses is the following: "I can doubt that my body exists; I cannot doubt that *I* exist; therefore my body is not essential to *my* existence."

This reasoning is clearly fallacious. Even if the premises are true the conclusion does not follow. If

5. *Ibid.*
6. *Ibid.,* p. 153, Meditation II.

I can doubt that a certain geometrical figure has the property $F$, but cannot doubt that it has the property $G$, it does not follow that $G$ does not entail $F$.

A more complex argument employed by Descartes is the following: "I have a clear and distinct perception of myself as a thinking and unextended thing, and of my body as an extended and unthinking thing; all things that I apprehend clearly and distinctly can be created by God in the manner I apprehend them; therefore I could exist without my body."

The first premise of this reasoning requires support. What assures Descartes that he has a clear and distinct perception of himself as a thinking but noncorporeal thing? His writings are not unmistakably clear on this point. There is some evidence that he had the following procedure in mind: since his aim was to find some property, $F$, which would be his essential nature, he made use of the following criterion or test: A property, $F$, constitutes my essential nature if it is necessarily the case *both* that if I am aware of $F$, then I am aware of myself (or of my existence, or that I exist), *and* if I am aware of myself (or ... et cetera), then I am aware of $F$. When *thinking* is substituted for $F$, both conditions of the criterion would appear to be satisfied. For both of the following propositions would seem to be necessarily true: if I am aware of thinking, I am aware that I exist; if I am aware that I exist, I am aware of thinking. If we substitute *body*, or *my body*, then the second condition is not satisfied. For it is not necessarily true that if I am aware that I exist, I am aware of my body. Thus it could seem to Descartes to be proved that he had a clear and distinct perception of himself as a thinking and unextended thing, and therefore (by the second of the two arguments stated above) that he was entitled to the conclusion that "this I (that is to say, my soul by which I am what I am), is entirely and absolutely distinct from my body, and can exist without it."[7]

A careful study of the workings of Descartes' criterion will show that the foregoing reasoning is invalid. Such a study will not be undertaken in this essay.[8] But even if none of Descartes' arguments in support of his mind-body dualism is valid, this does not disprove the dualism. Familiar facts would seem to support it. People have thoughts, make decisions and experience feelings, without there being any known physical occurrences corresponding to these mental occurrences. This would seem to present a case for the independence of mind and body.

It would be useful to clarify what Descartes meant by the separateness of mind and body. He believed that in actual fact a human being is an "intimate union" of mind and body. In saying that *I* (or my mind, or my soul) am separate and distinct from my body, he meant to be speaking only of what is *possible*. As far as the *concepts* of *myself* and *my body* are concerned, I could exist without a body. Descartes did not mean merely that I, having dwelt in a

7. *Ibid.*, p. 190, Meditation VI.
8. It is undertaken in my article "Descartes' Proof that His Essence Is Thinking," *Philosophical Review*, Vol. 74, No. 3, July 1965.

union with my body for some years, might be separated from it and yet survive in a disembodied condition. He meant that I might have existed without
*ever* having had a body. In that state what would my
mental life have been like? Logically speaking, it
could have been the same as it is and has been. For
my nature is to doubt, understand, affirm, deny, will,
imagine, and feel. As a bodiless mind I would do
those things. My mental acts, and the contents of my
consciousness, could be identical with what they are
in my actual embodied condition. In a sense even my
sensations could be the same, even though their apparent bodily locations and bodily causes would be
illusory. The history of my thoughts, desires, voli-
tions, emotions, and sensations might be just what
it has been, even if I was, and had always been, noncorporeal.

Sometimes the interest of readers of Descartes
declines when they come to understand that his doctrine of the separateness of mind and body does not
mean an actual separation, but only the conceptual
possibility of separation. This should not be so.
Philosophy is as much interested in the possible as
in the actual. Furthermore, the implications of this
possibility, if it is genuine, are of incomparable
significance. Descartes' dualism is a troubling beacon
around which the thoughts of subsequent philosophers have circled, both attracted and repelled.

Do we understand what it would mean for me to
have thoughts and desires, or to make decisions, if
I had been forever noncorporeal? Could there be a

distinction between *you* and *me*—a concept of *different selves?* If I had always been disembodied how would I have acquired the concepts on which my thinking turns? What would it mean for me to have a *correct* understanding of those concepts, as contrasted with an incorrect one?

In order to fully appraise the Cartesian doctrine of the separateness of mind and body, one would have to explore such topics as the nature of mental acts, the principles governing the identity and difference of persons, and the nature of concepts.

If disembodied mind is a possibility, although not a fact, then how are we to conceive of the actual relationship of body and mind? Is it to be understood purely in *causal* terms? Or possibly as a mere correlation? Could the actual correspondences between our mental contents and our bodily behavior have been entirely different? If so, how do I know that the same correlations, or causal connections, that hold in my case, hold true for other persons? What are the connections between speech and language, on the one hand, and mental contents, on the other? How do we succeed in conveying to one another our thoughts and experiences. Or do we? How can words refer to the various items of mental content? How can it be brought about that different people *mean* the same things by the words "thinking," "fear," and "hunger"? Do we *know* that they do? *How* do we know it? The Cartesian doctrine of separateness gives rise to these severely difficult problems of epistemology.

### 3. Impressions and Ideas

Descartes says virtually nothing about how language and speech are related to mental contents. But his conception of this was undoubtedly the same one that dominated British empiricism, and was expounded at length by John Locke. Let us turn to this conception.

In thinking, we employ ideas (concepts). How do we get them? Locke answers, from *experience*. Here he differs from Descartes, who held that this could not be true even of our idea of a material body. For *infinity* is an ingredient of our concept of a body. We conceive of a body (for example, a piece of wax) to be capable of an infinite number of alterations of shape and size. Experience could not have presented us with the perception of an infinity of changes. Our concept of an infinite must be possessed by us innately.

According to Locke our ideas have two sources: external sense and internal sense. Our sense organs are stimulated by external things, producing in us perceptions or sensations. These produce in us such ideas as soft and hard, bitter and sweet, heat and cold. Another class of ideas is obtained by our perception of the operations of our own minds. For example, we *remember* some sensations we have got from external sense, and by observing this operation of remembering we derive our idea of *memory*.

And such are *perception, thinking, doubting, believing, reasoning, knowing, willing,* and all the different actings of our own minds;—which we being conscious of, and observing in ourselves, do from these receive into our understandings as distinct ideas as we do from bodies affecting our senses. This source of ideas every man has wholly in himself: and though it be not sense, as having nothing to do with external objects, yet it is very like it, and might properly enough be called *internal sense*.[9]

Thus our whole stock of *simple* ideas is obtained from either the influence of external material things upon us, or from the mind's taking notice of its own acts and passions. It is "not in the power of the most exalted wit, or enlarged understanding, by any quickness or variety of thought, to *invent* or *frame* one new simple idea in the mind," that has not been taken in by one of these ways.[10] These simple ideas are joined together in manifold ways to produce complex ideas.

Hume had a similar conception. We receive impressions of heat or cold, thirst or hunger, pleasure or pain. The mind makes images or copies of these impressions, which are called *ideas*. These ideas give rise in the mind to feelings of desire or hope or fear. The mind in turn produces copies of these new feelings. Thus comes into being another set of ideas, largely the same as those that Locke holds to proceed from "internal sense."[11]

9. John Locke, *Essay Concerning Human Understanding*, ed. A. C. Fraser (Oxford, 1894), Bk. II, Ch. 1, Sec. 4.

10. *Ibid.*, Sec. 2.

11. Hume, *A Treatise of Human Nature*, ed. L. A. Selby-Bigge (Oxford, 1888), Bk. I, Part 1, Sec. 2.

## 4. Ideas as the Mind's Immediate Objects

For Locke, external and internal sense are "the windows by which light is let" into the bare, "dark room" of the mind. He thinks of the latter as being "not much unlike a closet wholly shut from light, with only some little opening left, to let in external visible resemblances, or ideas of things without."[12]

Locke speaks of ideas not only as "resemblances" of external things, but also as "pictures" and "patterns." Hume says that ideas are "images" of impressions. Descartes, too, speaks of ideas as "images": "Of my thoughts some are, so to speak, images of the things, and to these alone is the title 'idea' properly applied; examples are my thought of a man or of a chimera, of heaven, of an angel, or (even) of God."[13]

A striking view shared by these philosophers is that these images, pictures, or patterns are the mind's only immediate objects. Locke says: "Since the mind, in all its thoughts and reasonings, hath no other immediate object but its own ideas, which it alone does or can contemplate, it is evident that our knowledge is only conversant about them."[14] Descartes does not express himself so plainly, but the same view is implied by his procedure. For after proving his own existence and finding himself

12. Locke, *Essay*, Bk. II, Ch. 11, Sec. 17.
13. Descartes, *Philosophical Works*, Vol. 1, p. 163, Meditation III.
14. Locke, *Essay*, Bk. IV, Ch. 1, Sec. 1.

stocked with many ideas, he undertakes to establish
the existence of an *external* world, by ingenious reasoning from the content of his own ideas. Hume says
that it is "universally allow'd' by philosophers, and
is besides pretty obvious of itself, that nothing is
ever really present with the mind but its perceptions
or impression and ideas."[15] Berkeley remarked that
"it is evident to any one who takes a survey of the
objects of human knowledge, that they are either
ideas actually imprinted on the senses; or else such
as are perceived by attending to the passions and
operations of the mind; or lastly, ideas formed by
help of memory and imagination—either compound-
ing, dividing, or barely representing those originally
perceived in the aforesaid ways."[16] Locke did not
seriously doubt the existence of an external physical world, corresponding in some measure to our
ideas. Descartes did question it and sought to prove
an external world from the nature of those ideas.
But Hume held that it is impossible for us even to
conceive of anything different from our ideas and
impressions.[17] An external world does not even make
sense.

The present essay is not concerned with the tradi-
tionally difficult problems of the existence and perception of an external world. But an essay on the
philosophy of mind should note how great philos-

15. Hume, *Treatise*, Bk. I, Part 2, Sec. 6.
16. George Berkeley, *The Principles of Human Knowledge,* Part
I, Sec. 1; *Works of Berkeley,* ed. G. Sampson (London, 1897), Vol.
1, p. 181.
17. Hume, *Treatise*, Bk. I, Part 2, Sec. 6.

ophers have conceived the nature of mind. We are confronted with the astonishing fact that the dominant tradition has agreed with Descartes that the human mind (or self, or soul) is in its essential nature not dependent on a physical world. Minds are pictured as bodiless things that are filled with thoughts, impressions, feelings, experiences. Living corporeal persons are thought of as animated by minds. But minds and their contents, in their intrinsic nature, do not *require* corporeal embodiment. The belief in the essential separateness of mind and body, far from being an eccentricity of Descartes, is a common assumption of the most articulate and influential philosophers of the past three centuries.

## 5. Words and Ideas

If we obtain our ideas from internal impressions and from the observation of our own mental operations, and if the immediate objects of the mind's awareness are solely its own ideas, definite consequences will follow in regard to the relation between *language* and the thoughts and feelings it conveys. Locke drew those consequences. Words are to be used as marks of ideas in the mind of the speaker: "Words, in their primary or immediate signification, stand for nothing but *the ideas in the mind of him that uses them.*"[18] Words have no natural connection with ideas but are made into signs by the arbitrary

18. Locke, *Essay*, Bk. III, Ch. 2, Sec. 2.

choices of men. Since words are labels of ideas, the ideas must be present before they are labeled: "In the beginning of languages, it was necessary to have the idea before one gave it the name."[19] Thus it would be a logical possibility that a human creature with a mind well-stocked with ideas should have failed, for some reason, to assign any marks to them. He would be occupied with thoughts and observations, but devoid of language. He would have many concepts but no words with which to express them.

Thus Locke conceives of language as standing in a purely *external* relation to thinking. He declares that words have two uses: first, for each of us to record his own thoughts; second, to communicate those thoughts to others. In the first use, "whereby, as it were, we talk to ourselves, any words will serve the turn. . . . A man may use what words he pleases to signify his own ideas to himself: and there will be no imperfection in them if he constantly uses the same sign for the same idea. . . . "[20] Locke's external conception of language involves not only the assumption that thinking could occur without language, but also that each of us could have used language *solely* to record his thoughts and experiences for himself alone. Locke says that we "suppose" our words both to be signs of the ideas in the minds of others, and also to stand for "the reality of things." But these suppositions, he seems to think, are extraneous to the meaning of words; for he goes

19. *Ibid.*, Ch. 5, Sec. 15.
20. *Ibid.*, Ch. 9, Sec. 2.

on to remark that "it is perverting the use of words, and brings unavoidable obscurity and confusion into their signification, whenever we make them stand for anything but those ideas we have in our own minds."[21]

If a man's thoughts "are all within his own breast, invisible and hidden from others,"[22] it would seem to be an acute problem whether different persons have the same or different thoughts. Locke does not totally ignore this question, but it does not worry him much. He remarks that if words are to serve for communication, it is necessary that "they excite in the hearer exactly the same idea they stand for in the mind of the speaker."[23] But he does not go into the problem of how this could be *known*. He believes that speech between persons is often at cross-purposes; but this is mainly due to words that stand for complex ideas. With regard to the names of simple ideas, he thinks there is nearly always agreement between persons, chiefly because the ideas they stand for are "each but one single perception."[24] The one and only "sure way" of making known to another person the meaning of the name of a single idea is to present to his senses something that will "produce it in his mind, and make him actually have the idea that word stands for."[25] But Locke does not consider how it can be determined, or what it can *mean*, that

21. *Ibid.*, Ch. 2, Sec. 5.
22. *Ibid.*, Sec. 1.
23. *Ibid.*, Ch. 9, Sec. 6.
24. *Ibid.*, Sec. 18.
25. *Ibid.*, Ch. 11, Sec. 14.

another person's "invisible and hidden" idea is the *same* as mine.

## 6. Inner Ostensive Definition

What do *minds* do? It is said that they think, believe, doubt, know, reason, will. These actions or "operations" are *by* them, or *in* them. According to Locke, we observe "in ourselves" these "actings of our own minds," and *this is how we learn* what thinking, doubting, remembering, believing, and so on, *are*. From observing those operations in ourselves we obtain ideas of them in our understanding. Locke calls this source of information "Reflection," for the reason that "the ideas it affords being such only as the mind gets by reflecting on its own operations within itself."[26] Perhaps it would be more appropriate to call it "introspection," that is, inward observation. The prevalence of the assumption that each of us must obtain his concepts of the mental in this way is one of the most curious facts in the history of modern philosophy. The chief rival of this assumption has been the view that we do not *obtain* these concepts; we just *have* them; they are innate. But for philosophers of an empiricist inclination it has seemed *a matter of course* that we learn from introspection what thinking, remembering, and perceiving are. Remembering goes on in me; I apprehend its nature, I give it a name; thereafter, I

26. *Ibid.*, Bk. II, Ch. 1, Sec. 4.

use the name whenever I wish to record for myself or report to others that I remembered a certain thing. You do the same. Each of us labels something that he does or that goes on in him, *remembering*. But the *something* in each of us is, of course, hidden from the other. These definitions we give ourselves are "ostensive." Instead of physically pointing we mentally fix our attention on a certain inner phenomenon, and we make an association between it and a word. The ostensive definitions are "private"; they take place in each one's mind; no one else can be aware of, can directly know, those phenomena in my mind that I name "thinking," "remembering," or "believing."

## 7. Inferring the Existence of Other Minds

The assumption that each of us obtains his concepts of the mental from introspection inevitably began to pose problems. If I learned the mental concepts from my own case (from what went on in *me*), it would seem that I need a solid justification for my conviction that the same phenomena (or the same kinds) occur in minds other than mine. One can even say that I need a rational basis for believing there *are* other minds. For it is assumed that the only mind of which I have *direct* knowledge is my own. Other minds must have, for me, an inferred status. What would be the nature of the inference?

It was natural to suppose that the inference would be based on *analogy*—that is, it would be based on my perception of similarities between myself and some other beings. J. S. Mill gave a representative formulation of the problem, and of its presumed solution. He put this question: "By what evidence do I know, or by what considerations am I led to believe, that there exist other sentient creatures; that the walking and speaking figures which I see and hear, have sensations and thoughts, or in other words, possess Minds?" Mill answered as follows:

I conclude that other human beings have feelings like me, because, first, they have bodies like me, which I know, in my own case, to be the antecedent condition of feelings; and because, secondly, they exhibit the acts, and other outward signs, which in my own case I know by experience to be caused by feelings. I am conscious in myself of a series of facts connected by a uniform sequence, of which the beginning is modifications of my body, the middle is feelings, the end is outward demeanor. In the case of other human beings I have the evidence of my senses for the first and last links of the series, but not for the intermediate link. I find, however, that the sequence between the first and the last is as regular and constant in those other cases as it is in mine. In my own case I know that the first link produces the last through the intermediate link, and could not produce it without. Experience, therefore, obliges me to conclude that there must be an intermediate link; which must either be the same in others as in myself, or a different one: I must either believe them to be alive, or to be automatons: and by believing them to be alive, that is, by supposing the link to be of the same nature as in the case of which I have experience, and which is in all other respects similar, I bring other human beings, as phenomena, under the same generalizations which I know by experience to be the true theory of my own existence.[27]

Mill and other sponsors of this reasoning have understood that it can give the existence of other minds a status that is no more solid than a probability. W. T. Stace, a proponent of the analogical argument, has put the matter like this:

> It has to be admitted, of course, that the argument from bodily behaviour—the only genuinely logical argument which exists—does not yield certainty, but gives only a probable conclusion. This, as is well known, is true of all analogical reasoning. There is no means by which I can be absolutely *certain* that any mind exists except my own.[28]

It may be questioned whether the reasoning can even yield a probability. I am supposed to infer from the occurrence of a sequence of phenomena in a single case (my own) to the probable occurrence of the same sequence in a multitude of other walking and speaking figures. It might be replied that this is not "induction from a single instance," because I am presented (always in my own case, of course) with a large number of three-termed sequences of phenomena—bodily modifications, conscious experience, bodily motion. Still, it will be true that the class of three-termed sequences observed by me will be

27. J. S. Mill, *An Examination of Sir William Hamilton's Philosophy*, 6th ed. (New York, 1889), pp. 243–244.

28. W. T. Stace, *The Theory of Knowledge and Existence* (Oxford, 1932), p. 196.

small in comparison with the class of sequences which are merely two-termed *as far as my observation can determine.* The number of cases in which I do *not* perceive any feeling or thought intervening between bodily modification and bodily motion (which is how it is when I observe other "figures") is vastly greater than the number in which I do. This ought to give the result that whenever I am presented with a new example of a sequence of bodily modification and bodily motion I should regard it as *improbable,* rather than as probable, that some thought, feeling, or perception intervened between modification and motion. Taken quite seriously as a piece of inductive reasoning, the argument from analogy is topsy-turvy.

There is another noteworthy feature of this supposed inductive inference to the existence of other minds. Mill raised a query about his evidence for believing that "the walking and speaking figures" which he sees and hears possess minds. What "figures" did he mean? If the answer were "people," then surely it has never been an *open question* whether *people* have thoughts and sensations. It is part of what we mean by "a person" that a person has thoughts and sensations. If Mill were to say that his "figures" were living human *bodies,* then it would have to be asked what a living human body is, if not the body of a living *person?* If so, then it is settled from the beginning that those "figures" have minds, and no place is left for an inductive inference. Douglas Long states the point as follows:

What we see around us are people; we see their bodies too, of course, but these are the bodies of living persons. We have not yet been told how to pick out living human bodies that *may or may not be the bodies of persons.* Unless this is explained, there is no reason to think that the concept of a living human body is not the same as the concept of the living body of a person or of the body of a living person. And if these are the same concept, the question whether or not such a body is that of a person is still not an open one.[29]

Mill and like-minded philosophers have a difficulty, apparently insurmountable, in trying to state a genuine question—a question to be settled by evidence, and to be dealt with (by each of us) through reasoning from analogy with our own case. I am to draw an analogy between myself and *what*—living human bodies that I see and hear? But the idea these philosophers suppose themselves to have, of a living human body that *might not* be the body of a person, is not intelligible.[30]

A somewhat similar point has been made by Peter Strawson. According to Mill, I start out from ''my own case.'' I observe correlations between *my* states of consciousness and the states of *my* body. Mill assumes that from the start I have the concept of *myself* as a subject of experience. But this must imply that from the start I have the concept of subjects of experience *other* than myself. If not, there would be no sense in thinking of the starting point

29. D. C. Long, ''The Philosophical Concept of A Human Body,'' *Philosophical Review*, Vol. 73, No. 3, July 1964, p. 325.
30. Cf. *ibid.*, p. 329.

as *my own* case. The very form of the philosophical problem, to which the argument from analogy is addressed, requires that the distinction between ascribing mental phenomena to *myself* and ascribing them to *others,* is already understood. As Strawson says:

> There is no sense in the idea of ascribing states of consciousness to oneself, or at all, unless the ascriber already knows how to ascribe at least some states of consciousness to others. So he cannot (or cannot generally) argue "from his own case" to conclusions about how to do this; for unless he already knows how to do this, he has no conception of *his own case.* . . .[31]

If I do not already know how and when, at least sometimes, to say that various mental predicates are true of *others,* I do not have a concept of subjects of experience other than myself. So then I do not have the concept of *myself* as a subject of experience. As Wittgenstein remarks: "If you logically exclude other people's having something, it loses its sense to say that *you* have it."[32] But this prevents the reasoning from an analogy with *my* case from even getting started.

On the other hand, if I have a grasp of the contrast between myself and others, as subjects of experience, there is then no place for the reasoning to go. That

31. P. F. Strawson, ''Persons,'' *Minnesota Studies in the Philosophy of Science,* Vol. 2, ed. H. Feigl, M. Scriven, and G. Maxwell (Minneapolis, 1958); reprinted in *Body and Mind,* ed. G. N. A. Vesey (London, 1964), p. 415. See also Strawson's book, *Individuals* (London, 1959), pp. 100–103.

32. Ludwig Wittgenstein, *Philosophical Investigations* (New York, 1953), Sec. 398; italics added.

the ostensible goal has already been obtained would be implicit in the starting point. A philosopher who intends to argue from analogy for the existence of other minds would have to be, as Long remarks, "in the position of being free to decide on the basis of evidence whether or not the 'bodies' he observes are those of people, and this would require in turn that he understand what a person is. But if he understood what a person is, he would be able to identify other human beings as people and the question would not really be open after all."[33]

There is something exceedingly curious in Mill's statement of the "problem of other minds." He asks whether "other human beings" have thoughts and sensations. But human beings are none other than people, and any things we believed to be incapable of thoughts or feelings we should refuse to call either "people" or "human beings." Another way in which Mill frames the problem is to ask whether other human beings are "alive," or whether they are "automatons." But obviously Mill wants to raise his question in reference to human beings who are alive, who walk and speak, not in reference to corpses. Also it is not evident what Mill could mean by asking whether other human beings are *automatons*. Could he be wondering whether they are artifacts? Or whether their interiors are filled with machinery?

These preliminary probings of the alleged problem

33. Long, *op. cit.*, p. 337.

of our evidence for the existence of other minds raise doubts as to whether it can be stated as a *meaningful* question. Mill wants to put the problem in terms of a certain class of things. How can he specify this class in such a way as to leave it an open question whether its members have thoughts and feelings? Not as the class of human beings, or of people. Not as the class of living human bodies (or "human figures"). For they are the bodies of people. Not as the class of those bodies that "resemble" *my* body. For many material objects, and also bodies of animals, resemble my body in various respects. The relevant and necessary features of resemblance would have to be spelled out to the point where it was clear that the membership of this class was limited to the bodies of other living *persons*. So none of these specifications would yield a class of beings with regard to which it was undetermined whether they have, or are the bodies of beings that have, thoughts and feelings. It does not appear that such a specification could be made.

## 8. Solipsism

A solipsist is one who affirms theses such as the following: "I am the only mind"; "I am the only thinker"; "All thoughts and experiences are my thoughts and experiences." But a man could say such things to himself who believed that he was the sole survivor of a hydrogen explosion, and he would not thereby be a solipsist. I shall understand a solipsist to be a philosopher who thinks that it does *not make sense,* is not meaningful, to suppose that there are thoughts or experiences other than his own.

Solipsism is often regarded as a laughable doctrine. In depreciation of it I have heard someone say that no great philosopher has been a solipsist. If this is so it is only due to a lack of rigor, or to a failure to develop consequences. The foundations of solipsism are in the systems of Descartes, Locke, Berkeley, and Hume, and in the assumptions of all those philosophers who hold that one's belief in the existence of other minds must be based on reasoning from analogy with one's own case.

Descartes' viewpoint implies not only that a human mind, with all its contents, could exist without ever being embodied but also that it could be lodged in a body unlike the human.

Logically speaking, there would be no limits with regard to the size, shape, material, or structure of the body in which it was lodged: a rock, a chair, a tree, or a turtle would be possibilities. Whether it had a bodily lodging and, if so, what kind, would be matters of purely contingent fact which could be otherwise. It would also be a contingent matter whether there were any correlations between the states of a mind and the condition, circumstances, and movements of its body. If there were correlations it would be a contingent matter what their nature was. Nothing could be ruled out. Another way of putting this view is to say that there are no *conceptual* connections between the contents of a mind and the states of its body. It could not be a part of the *meaning* of a mind's feeling anger or pain that its body was disposed thus and so.

Locke's endorsement of introspection as the process by which each person or self obtains his concepts of mental "operations" shows that he accepts the Cartesian position. I learn what thinking, remembering, and so on, are, by observation of what goes on in my mind, not by observing my own bodily conditions and movements. Since my knowledge of the nature of the mental operations is separate from my knowledge of the states of my body, the nature of those operations is presumed to be independent (logically speaking) of bodily states. The correlations, if there are any, between the acts and contents of my mind, and the states and doings of my body, will be entirely contingent, and will have to be found out by my own observations *after* I have formed my ideas of the mental phenomena.

It is evident that those philosophers who think it necessary to reason from analogy to the existence of other minds are committed to the Cartesian-Lockean assumption of a conceptual gap between the mental and the physical. Mill, for example, supposes that, first of all, he learns from inner perception what thoughts and sensations are. Subsequently he takes note of correlations between those inner mental occurrences and his bodily circumstances and movements. He observes similar physical facts in the case of other beings, and infers that they have an inward life similar to his own.

All of these philosophers are united in the belief that our understanding of the concepts of the mental is separated from our knowledge of the physical world and, more particularly, from our knowledge of the bodily circumstances and behavior of both ourselves and other persons. Let us assume that this belief is true, in order to see how solipsism emerges from it. Each of us, in his own case, comprehends the nature of the mental entirely apart from any knowledge of the physical aspects of a person. I observe anger in myself, and understand what it is, and am able to affirm that *I* am angry. But will I even be able to conceive that some *other* being is angry? A rock or a tree, for example? Would I know what it *meant* to say that those things were angry?

One might reply that of course it would be meaningless to attribute feelings to trees or rocks, but not meaningless to attribute them to other *people*. But the problem here is, in part, whether I can understand the supposition that there are *other people*. I am supposed to have learned from introspection what thinking and anger are. I am surrounded by bodies, some similar to mine, some different. If there is a conceptual gap between the physical and the mental, then the differences between those *bodies* will be irrelevant. It should be just as easy, therefore, and just as difficult, for me to ascribe anger or pain to a stone as to any other *body*. Or should it be put like this: I conceive that the stone has a mind or soul, and I attribute anger to that soul. Why cannot a stone have a soul if a human body can have one?

If the Cartesian doctrine of a conceptual gap between the physical and the mental were true, it
would make *as much* sense to attribute thoughts and
feelings to a chair as to something that has the
human form. Now, should I believe that this chair
on which I sit feels pain or that it does not? There
is an inclination to think the latter: but with what
justification? Is it that the chair *shows no signs* of
pain? But what *would be* a sign of pain in a chair?
Is there anything a chair *could* do or undergo, which
we should want to regard as a sign of pain? With a
person or a dog it is clear what a sign of pain is, but
not with a chair.[34] Thus we cannot support our inclination to say that chairs do not feel pain. Perhaps
what we should say is that *we do not know* whether
chairs feel pain. We do not know when a chair should
be said to be suffering. We do not know what an
*expression* of anger or an *occasion* for anger would
be. Although the sentences "This chair feels pain,"
"This chair is angry" are English sentences, and
English speakers understand the words that compose
them, there is a sense in which these sentences are
not understood. This sense is the following: English
speakers do not know in what circumstances it should
be affirmed or denied that a chair feels pain or anger.
We do not know when these things would be true or
false. Although the sentences are "well-formed," no
one knows how to apply them to reality. In truth,

34. In a recent lecture on electronic computers I heard the speaker
remark that the machines in current use show no signs of consciousness!

they *have* no application to reality. They do not even express *possible* states of affairs.

This shows that it is misleading to say, as we proposed above, that "we do not know" whether chairs feel pain or anger. It is not a matter of ignorance. Quite the contrary. This "not knowing" is actually the perception that it would be meaningless to inquire whether a chair is angry.

If the viewpoint of Descartes and Locke were correct, I should not be entitled to regard other human figures any differently from rocks or chairs. If I obtained my concepts of the mental from introspection, and if there are no conceptual ties between the physical aspects and behavior of anything and its mental life, then I shall not know how to apply mental predicates to anything other than myself. It will be as meaningless to suppose that another human being is angry as that this chair is. If I think matters through, I shall end up a solipsist.

## 9.  The Living Human Being

Various objections to this conclusion will be felt. It might be said: "I can imagine that a stone or chair has consciousness, and so I must be able to do the same in regard to another human figure." It is true that a certain play of imagination is possible. One can imagine intelligible speech coming from a rock; and in a fairy tale a chair can be happy or dejected. But, as Wittgenstein remarks, these imaginings establish nothing of philosophical importance.[35] They have no tendency to prove that a thinking rock is a possibility. What would show that the rock was *speaking* (and was not merely a source of sound)? What would establish that the rock *understood* the sounds that came from it?[36] In a cartoon a chair is endowed with an expressive face and humanlike movements. Our concepts of feeling and experience can seem to get a grip on a chair only in so far as we invest it with something that approximates the human form and behavior. As Wittgenstein says: "Only of a living human being and what resembles (behaves like) a living human being can one say: it has sensations; it sees; is blind; hears; is deaf; is conscious or unconscious."[37] When we attribute sensation or thinking to lower animals, we are using the living human being as our standard of comparison. The more distant the animal life is from this standard the less confident become our ascriptions of thinking or sensation. "We say only of a human being, and what is like one, that it thinks."[38]

It might be thought that this result is identical with the outcome of the argument from analogy and therefore not a criticism of it. This is not so. The argument from analogy proceeds on the assumption that each of us derives his concepts of the mental from taking note of the happenings in his own mind.

35. Wittgenstein, *op. cit.*, Sec. 390.
36. This point is discussed in my *Knowledge and Certainty* (Englewood Cliffs, N.J., 1963), pp. 134–136.
37. Wittgenstein, *op. cit.*, Sec. 281.
38. *Ibid.*, Sec. 360.

The associating of these mental occurrences with the human figure and behavior is done subsequently, and does not enter into the *meaning* of the mental attributions. The association is contingent. If my body had been a tree, I should have associated consciousness, first of all, with the shapes, bendings, and sighings of trees, and with human figures only insofar as they resembled trees. But these would only be *associations*. My understanding of the concepts of mind would be independent of my particular corporeal lodging. My belief that other human bodies are mind-inhabited would be due to association or to induction. The associations and inductions could have been different, but the concepts of thought, volition, perception, et cetera, would have been the same. For I derived them from my inner experience.

In opposition to this view it needs to be said that the living human being is as essential to our concepts of the mental as the chessboard is to chess. One concept we have is of someone's doing something *willingly* or *unwillingly*. There are the related concepts of *reluctantly, sullenly, under protest, obediently, cheerfully, eagerly*, and so on. Just as an angry chair is a senseless notion (that is, one we do not know how to apply), so is the notion of a tree's scraping its branches *reluctantly*. One thing lacking is a context of activities, interests, goals, frustrations, in terms of which a tree's "reluctance" would make sense. The possibility of such a context presupposes something approximating the human figure, countenance, and behavior. A person can *act out* reluctance, but we should not know how it could be represented by a tree.

A living human being is our paradigm of one who thinks, feels, and perceives. It provides our standard of comparison, in terms of which nonhuman creatures are judged to have more or less of mental life. Nothing could be more wrongheaded than to suppose that one's acceptance of other human beings as conscious creatures is done by association or by inductive inference. To think this way would be to throw away one's yardstick.

## 10. Obtaining Concepts by Introspection

The philosophical belief that the living, corporeal, human being is not logically essential to our concepts of the mental can probably be discredited only by undermining the assumption that we can obtain those concepts through introspection. Wittgenstein accomplishes this in the *Investigations,* thereby making perhaps the greatest single contribution to the philosophy of mind.

One strategy Wittgenstein employs is to encourage us to study closely *what actually happens* when some particular mental phenomenon occurs. For example, you are trying to remember where you left your car key, and suddenly you do remember; or you are puzzled as to how to read a map, and suddenly you understand it; or you are hesitating between boating and gardening, and suddenly you decide between them. The sudden remembering, or understanding,

or decision are mental events. They are occurrences
at a certain moment of time.

If the assumption were correct that introspection
teaches us what deciding, understanding, and so
forth, are, it ought to be the case that *at the moment*
of decision or understanding (or at least in subsequent reflection) we could *single out* the events of
deciding or understanding from all of the accompany-
ing phenomena. But can we do this? Wittgenstein
invites us to consider the following example:

A writes a series of numbers down; B watches him and
tries to find a law for the sequence of numbers. If he
succeeds he exclaims: "Now I can go on!"—So this
capacity, this understanding, is something that makes
its appearance in a moment. So let us try and see what
it is that makes its appearance here.—A has written
down the numbers 1, 5, 11, 19, 29; at this point B
says he knows how to go on. What happened here?
Various things may have happened; for example,
while A was slowly putting one number after another,
B was occupied with trying various algebraic formulae
on the numbers which had been written down. After
A had written the number 19 B tried the formula
$a_n = n^2 + n - 1$; and the next number confirmed his
hypothesis.

Or again, B does not think of formulae. He watches
A writing his numbers down with a certain feeling of
tension, and all sorts of vague thoughts go through his
head. Finally he asks himself: "What is the series of
differences?" He finds the series 4, 6, 8, 10 and says:
Now I can go on.

Or he watches and says "Yes I know *that* series"—
and continues it, just as he would have done if A had
written down the series 1, 3, 5, 7, 9.—Or he says noth-

ing at all and simply continues the series. Perhaps he
had what may be called the sensation "that's easy!"
(Such a sensation is, for example, that of a light quick
intake of breath, as when one is mildly startled.)[39]

Now if we ask *what* the sudden understanding was, it
is evident that the answer is not that it consisted in
B's thinking of the formula: "For it is perfectly
imaginable that the formula should occur to him and
that he should nevertheless not understand."[40] One
could pronounce, or see in one's mind, a certain
formula without knowing how to use it. Nor can the
answer be that B's sudden understanding consisted
in his thinking of the next few numbers in the
sequence, nor in his writing them down: for someone
might accidentally get the first few numbers right
but fail to understand the series. Nor can it consist
in the sudden relief of tension. And so on. We see
that none of these phenomena, which Wittgenstein
calls "characteristic *accompaniments*" of sudden
understanding, *is* the understanding. We cannot put
our finger on *anything* occurring at the moment of
understanding, which *is* the understanding. *The
understanding itself is not anything we can single
out or fix our attention on.*

This technique of "dissolving" various mental
processes and occurrences does not prove that there
is no such thing as sudden deciding, or understand-

---

39. *Ibid.*, Sec. 151. Also see the notes dictated by Wittgenstein and
published posthumously under the title *The Blue and the Brown Books*
(Oxford, 1958), pp. 112–116.
40. Wittgenstein, *Investigations*, Sec. 152.

ing, or remembering. Obviously there is nothing wrong with saying that someone suddenly remembered where he put his keys. What is proved is that there is not, in addition to the characteristic accompaniments, another occurrence, which is the remembering itself, and on which one's attention can dwell.

Perhaps it is too much to say that this is *proved*. A philosopher may still believe that he does detect something there—something that is intangible and indescribable. William James, for example, in speaking of *the intention of saying something before one has said it,* declares that such an intention is "an absolutely distinct state of consciousness," having "a nature of its own of the most positive sort." Yet, he thinks, one cannot *describe* its nature; one can only label it as the intention *to-say-so-and-so*.[41]

Is it true that whenever one makes a remark, in normal conversation, the intention of saying it existed as a definite state of consciousness before one said it? Suppose there were preparations for a card game and you said to the other players, "The pack of cards is on the table." Now if you dwell on this sentence in your imagination, and silently rehearse those words, you may feel that something is going on in your consciousness that has "a nature of its own of the most positive sort." But how often do you say or think a sentence to yourself before you utter it? This is comparatively infrequent. It might happen if the words belonged to a secret code and your

41. James, *Principles*, Vol. I, p. 253.

utterance would be a signal of momentous consequence. Or if you were about to appear before an audience to speak some lines in a play. But in the normal course of conversation, discussion, questioning, disagreement, urging, insisting—you certainly do not rehearse, or even weigh, your words before you pronounce them. (There is not time!) Yet if you were interrupted while speaking, you could later state exactly what you had previously intended to say. It was true that you had the intention to say so-and-so before you said it, but false that there was some definite state of consciousness corresponding to that intention. How could we have even thought there was?

Wittgenstein suggests that when we philosophize about the nature of intention, understanding, recognition, remembering, deciding, and so on, we fix our attention on ourselves in a curious way. In order to observe what deciding is, we decide to do something (for example, to stand, or sit), and we try to concentrate on ourselves at the same time—stare at ourselves, so to speak. We do this because we have the prior conviction that deciding must be a definite mental event, "of a positive nature," which we can observe. By this concentration we do indeed create a special "atmosphere," a peculiar experience. This makes us think we have brought *deciding* under observation. But all we have done is to gaze at ourselves in an unusual way.[42] We have no grounds for

---

42. See Wittgenstein, *The Blue and the Brown Books*, pp. 158–167.

thinking that always or usually when we make a decision some special experience occurs. Recollection of normal cases will show us that this is not so. James (like Locke) believed that the intention to say a certain thing must be something one can perceive inwardly. Undoubtedly he "verified" this belief by dwelling with peculiar concentration on some sentence that he was about to utter. What he produced was the curious self-absorbed condition of a philosopher who is trying to exhibit to his introspection the nature of some mental state.

## 11. Tangible and Intangible Mental Phenomena

When we study "what happens" when we make a decision, suddenly understand how to solve a problem, say something and *mean* it, think of what we are saying, remember an engagement, become convinced of something, we are not able to describe, or even to fix our attention on, the phenomenon itself, *in addition to* its characteristic accompaniments or manifestations. If I describe what happened at the moment I decided to stop work and to go for a swim, the tangible occurrences I can mention are such things as my saying the words "All right; I will go," my starting toward the door, my having a visual image of a lake, my thinking to myself, "A swim will be good for me." I may be led to say that I cannot get hold of the deciding itself—it eludes me. The conclusion ought to have been that I was mistaken in supposing that the act of deciding would be that sort of thing. I should have realized that deciding has no "experience content" (*Erlebnisinhalt*).

> Meaning is as little an experience as intending. But what distinguishes them from experience?—They have no experience-content. For the contents (images for instance) which accompany and illustrate them are not the meaning or intending.[43]

In contrast, there are mental phenomena that do have "experience-content": for example, bodily sensations, afterimages, and at least some mental images. You can pay more or less attention to your headache while it is going on. And you can *describe the headache itself*—which is something you cannot do with deciding or intending. Unlike deciding, remembering, and so on, bodily sensations do not "dissolve" under this kind of scrutiny. One can say, with justification, that a pain in a limb is something definite, *concrete*—something with "a positive nature of its own." In addition to the bodily movements, grimaces, exclamations, which accompany and express it, one can attend to the sensation itself and report its cessation or continuation, its waxing and waning, its changes of quality.

If we return to Locke's belief that we get our ideas of mental phenomena by "observing in ourselves" the "actings of our own minds," we see that this belief loses plausibility when the phenomena are of the kind that "dissolve." An increase of philosophical sophistication makes us see that we cannot have

43. Wittgenstein, *Investigations*, pp. 216–217.

obtained these concepts by inward observation; for we cannot succeed in picking out those acts and processes, and therefore we can no longer believe that they ever were objects of inner perception. But Locke's belief might still be held in respect to mental phenomena of the "concrete" kind; for example, sensations and images.

It is interesting to note that Bertrand Russell once held that "the stuff of our mental life . . . consists wholly of sensations and images."[44] "Thoughts, beliefs, desires, pleasures, pains and emotions are all built up out of sensations and images alone."[45] Speaking of introspective observation, Russell said: "I think that observation shows us nothing that is not composed of sensations and images."[46]

Thus it seems likely that Russell felt the difference between what we have called "tangible" and "intangible" mental phenomena. The tangible ones (sensations and images) are truly discernible by introspection. They are regarded as the *real* or *ultimate* mental phenomena. Intangible ones are "constructions" out of them.

We can learn from this distinction that Wittgenstein's technique of dissolving mental phenomena (for example, recognizing, inferring, understanding) cannot be sufficient to overthrow Locke's doctrine that our concepts of the mental are obtained by

44. Bertrand Russell, *The Analysis of Mind* (New York, 1921, 5th impression, 1949), p. 109.
45. *Ibid.*, p. 121.
46. *Ibid.*, p. 117.

introspection. Making Russell's distinction between "ultimate" and "reducible" mental occurrences, a philosopher could still hold a modified version of Locke's doctrine. It would not even have to be a modification of the general theory. For the occurrences that, in themselves, can be objects of introspective attention (sensations and images), and are directly describable, would be held to yield the *simple* mental concepts ("simple ideas of reflection"), from which we build the "complex" ones. The only disagreement with Locke would be to deny that such concepts as *"remembrance, discerning, reasoning, judging, knowledge, faith,"* are "simple ideas of reflection."[47] The range of complex, analyzable, ideas would be far greater than Locke had supposed. But the origin of our concepts of the mental, *as a whole,* would be from introspection, just as Locke believed.

Thus something more radical than the technique of dissolving mental phenomena must be devised, if we are to avoid the doctrine of the derivation of concepts from introspection, with its solipsistic consequences. This, too, is undertaken by Wittgenstein.

## 12. Using a Picture

Locke and Hume thought that we obtain concepts from "experience." We experience a sensation (or "impression") of red color, and we draw out of the

47. Locke, *Essay*, Bk. II, Ch. 6.

sensation, in some way, the concept of red. On their
view the concept might be likened to a diaphanous
membrane which we peel off from the sensation and
store in our minds, where it serves as a pattern to
guide our future recognitions. We obtain "simple"
concepts of mental occurrences in the same way. If
pain or anger or thinking are "simple ideas," they
are derived from inward occurrences of pain, anger,
and thinking. Once we have these concepts we can
give them *names*. Ideas come first, names later.

Wittgenstein remarks of a similar conception of
St. Augustine's that it is "as if the child came into
a strange country and did not understand the language of the country; that is, as if it already had a
language, only not this one. Or again: as if the child
could already *think*, only not yet speak."[48]

This conception prevents one from perceiving the
threat of solipsism. From a particular feeling I have
drawn off a pattern or picture or model of that feeling. I give it the name "pain." Why should there
be any difficulty in my *conceiving* that others feel
pain? For I possess a model, an exemplar, a "copy"
(Hume's word) of pain as it might exist *anywhere*.
I know "what it would be like" for another person
to have it. He would have *this:* (here I indicate my
exemplar). It may be difficult or impossible for me to
find out whether he has it: but I know what it *means*
to say he does.

A question needs to be asked. Cannot a picture,

48. Wittgenstein, *Investigations*, Sec. 32.

model, or sample be used in various ways? Cannot it represent different things? What will be the difference between its being used to represent one thing rather than another? Wittgenstein raises this question about samples of colors:

> When someone defines the names of colours for me by pointing to samples and saying "This colour is called 'blue', this 'green' . . ." this case can be compared in many respects to putting a table in my hands, with the words written under the colour-samples.—Though this comparison may mislead in many ways.—One is now inclined to extend the comparison: to have understood the definition means to have in one's mind an idea of the thing defined, and that is a sample or picture. So if I am shown various different leaves and told "This is called a 'leaf,' " I get an idea of the shape of a leaf, a picture of it in my mind.—But what does the picture of a leaf look like when it does not show us any particular shape, but "what is common to all shapes of leaf"? Which shade is the "sample in my mind" of the colour green—the sample of what is common to all shades of green?
>
> "But might there not be such 'general' samples? Say a schematic leaf, or a sample of *pure* green?"— Certainly there might. But for such a schema to be understood as a *schema*, and not as the shape of a particular leaf, and for a slip of pure green to be understood as a sample of all that is greenish and not as a sample of pure green—this in turn resides in the way the samples are used.[49]

Similar questions should be raised about my supposed sample of pain. What is to prevent me from

---

49. *Ibid.*, Sec. 73.

taking it (whatever *it* is) as a sample of "mental" pain—grief or anguish, for example, instead of physical pain? Why could I not even use it to represent *relief* from pain? As Wittgenstein remarked, we might teach someone what "modesty" is by indicating a person of haughty bearing. Or I might explain to a child the meaning of making his bed "neatly," by pointing at his disorderly bed and saying *"Not like this."* Or consider the possibility of someone's using a sample of a certain color in order to select materials of the *complementary* color.

Thus if I did abstract a pattern, picture, or sample of pain from a feeling, it would not follow that I used it as a representation of *pain*. Furthermore, if I did use it as a representation of pain, it would not follow that I used it correctly, or that I arrived at the right results. I may lose my way on forest trails even if I consult a map. I may not know how to read it. Whatever the sample of pain was, I could go wrong in my use of it. Why should it be assumed that if I am presented a copy of something, I shall know how to make use of it? This is not true of the maps, drawings, or models that we can hold in our hands and study. Why should it be true of the copies or patterns *in the mind?*

If a picture is going to be useful to me, I have to know what to do with it. This is not guaranteed by the mere fact that the picture is placed in my hand, or mind. If a child is given a footrule, he may not know how to measure with it. He may think that its width, not its length, is equal to a foot. Or he may "measure" in some unheard of way. He believes he knows what a foot is, but he is wrong. If he were asked what a foot is he would reply, "It is the same as *this*" (pointing at a footrule). His ostensive definition is correct: but still he does not know what a foot is.

The assumption of Descartes, Locke, and Hume (an assumption that is enormously attractive to all of us) that to possess a concept (idea) is to have a picture or copy in the mind, is thus seen to be inadequate. It does not solve the problem. Even if someone had a mental copy of pain and told himself that to have pain means to have *this* (indicating his copy), he might still have no mastery of the concept. He might not know when to ascribe pain either to himself or to another person.

A mental picture is not sufficient for understanding: but also it is not necessary. For how am I to know that I am using the *right* mental picture? Must I first compare it with another mental picture—and so on, *ad infinitum?* Wittgenstein asks us to consider the order "*Imagine* a red patch," and he remarks: "You are not tempted in this case to think that *before* obeying you must have imagined a red patch to serve you as a pattern for the red patch which you were ordered to imagine."[50] You cannot always resort to a mental pattern in order to identify a mental pattern, for this would require an infinite regress of comparisons. But if I can know that I have

50. Wittgenstein, *The Blue and the Brown Books*, p. 3; cf. *Investigations*, Sec. 239.

an image of red, *without* having compared the image with a pattern, why cannot I know that this *paper* is red without having made a comparison? A copy or sample in the mind cannot be a logically necessary condition of my being able to make identifications.

Our philosophical assumption that we obtain our concepts of mental occurrences and operations "from our own case" begins to lose its charm. A pattern or copy, so derived, cannot be *required,* and will not *suffice,* for understanding a concept.

## 13.  Knowing What Pain Is

It may be felt that the notion that I obtain, from my own experience, a copy, image, or sample of pain is too crude. What I do get from my own case is a knowledge of *what pain is.* The same with imagery, seeing and hearing, calculating in one's head, and so on.

What does it mean "to know what pain is"? Do *you* know what pain is? Do *I* know? I cannot *define* the word "pain." If I said that "pain" means a "disagreeable feeling," this would not even be true. Dizziness is a disagreeable feeling, but it is not pain. Weakness or lethargy can be unpleasant. Something cold, damp, and wriggling might produce a disagreeable sensation, which was nevertheless not painful.

It might be thought that "knowing what pain is" consists in seeing what is *common* to various pains. But what *is* common to the pain of sunburn and of indigestion? Do not say "They are similar," for our

question is, *how* are they similar? If you say "One
wants to be rid of both," this is true: but it is also
true of anxiety, uncertainty, and fear. So this common feature is not what pain *consists* of. On reflection, it becomes obvious that we are not going to be
able to specify any feature common to all painful
sensations and in which their being painful consists.
We are no better off here than we would be if someone asked us to say what different shades of blue
have in common; or what mental strain and physical
strain have in common.[51]

One is inclined to say "From my own experience
of pain I grasp the essential thing." But what *is* the
essential thing? We have no reason to think that
there is an essential nature of pain—something common to all pain that makes it pain.

Some things are essential (that is, required) for
it to be true that a person understands the concept
of pain. One is that he should be able to say of himself (and be right) that he feels pain or does not feel
pain. Another is that he should be able to recognize
the characteristic expressions of pain and should
know the behavioral consequences of pain, in other
human beings. Still another is that he should have
a certain attitude toward the sufferings of other
persons.

Someone might object: "Even if those things are
required, you have left out the most important thing,
namely, the actual experiencing of pain. If a person

51. Wittgenstein, *Investigations,* Sec. 72; *The Blue and the Brown
Books,* pp. 129–134.

had not undergone *that,* he would not understand the concept; for he would not know *what* pain is."

## 14. The Man Who Has Never Felt Pain

Let us suppose that a grown man, Robinson, was abnormal in the respect of having never felt pain. Let us also suppose that through training and observation he had come to be able to identify the behavior and expressions of pain in others and thus to be able to verify that some other person does or does not feel pain. He can do this as well as you or I can. Let us further suppose that Robinson shows as much concern for the suffering of others as does any normal person. If someone is writhing in pain, Robinson will be anxious to comfort and relieve him. On the other hand, if he is angry with or dislikes someone he may deliberately inflict pain on him. In short, Robinson knows the "value" of pain, as well as possessing a normal ability to determine whether others feel pain.

Someone may remark that Robinson still does not know what the word "pain" means in *his own* case. But let us imagine that Robinson can simulate pain-behavior skillfully. He is an amateur actor and can be relied on to give a convincing representation of a suffering person. In a play, his words "The pain is dreadful" are connected with the right (simulated) behavior. Are we still entitled to be confident that Robinson does not understand the application of the word "pain" to his own case?

It may be objected that since Robinson is only pretending, it has not yet been proved that he would know when the sentence ''I feel pain'' expressed a *true* proposition about himself; and this could never be proved. Is this so? Let us suppose that Robinson is under medical treatment the aim of which is to provide him, for his own protection, with normal sensations of pain. Serums are injected in the hope of obtaining a pain reaction. But after each injection Robinson says ''No, I don't feel any pain''; and the rest of his behavior shows that what he says is true. Thus we have excellent grounds for believing that he *understands* the meaning of the sentence ''I do *not* feel pain.'' If this is so, must he not understand its contradictory?

We made the assumption that Robinson does not feel pain. This entails that he does not ever say ''I feel pain,'' when this is true. But it cannot follow that he does not understand this sentence. I have never been in Brazil, and so have never been in the position to say ''I am in Brazil,'' when this was true: but of course I understand the sentence.

We are dealing with the strong inclination to think that it is logically, or conceptually, impossible that a person who has never felt pain should know the meaning of the word ''pain.'' This inclination is hard pressed to defend itself. Our hypothetical Robinson demonstrates, in many ways, a thorough understanding of the word—as good an understanding as anyone has. As a matter of contingent fact, it may be that a person with Robinson's incapacity for feeling pain would not feel any compassion for suffering persons or be able to simulate, convincingly, agonies of pain. Just as it may be true, humanly speaking, that a person who had never had any inclination towards vanity would be puzzled by displays of vanity in other persons and would be liable to take it for something else. But the view I am disputing says that as a matter of conceptual possibility, not of contingent fact, someone who had never experienced pain *could not* understand the word. If this *were* so, there would have to be something self-contradictory or incoherent in my total description of Robinson's case. But this is not so. No inconsistency can be detected. Each additional assumption was compatible with what had been assumed previously.

One might want to ask "Why should Robinson have compassion for other persons if he has never felt pain?" But do we really know why anyone is compassionate? There are big differences between people in this respect. Do we have to believe that the most sympathetic people are the ones who have suffered the most severe pain?

## 15.  A Comparison with Blindness

We might think that Robinson's incapacity for pain is like blindness. "Surely a blind person does not know the meaning of the words 'red' and 'blue': in Robinson's case the same holds for the word 'pain.'" This comparison is worth examining. Of course a blind man could know the physical theory of colors. Also he could know how the different colors are related: for example, which are the primary colors, whether orange is *between* red and yellow, and so on. It may be remarked that this is knowledge *about* colors, not knowledge by *acquaintance* with colors, and that the latter is necessary for knowing the *meaning* of the color words. Let us see what truth there is in this idea.

There is something a blind man cannot do. He cannot assign the right names to colors *by sight*. He lacks a certain ability. When a normal child begins to manifest this ability, we call this "learning the names of the colors." *In this sense* a blind man does not learn and does not know the names of colors. This much can be said in favor of the claim that he "does not know the meaning" of color words.

But there is no parallel for this in the case of Robinson. He is not lacking a normal ability in the use of language. He applies the word "pain" to other people in accordance with the ordinary criteria. And he employs the word correctly in his own case. He does not ever make the mistake of saying "I do not feel pain," when he does feel pain, or of saying "I feel pain," when he does not. If a man is blind there will be colors directly in front of him which he will be unable to name and describe. But Robinson does not have pains which he cannot name and describe.

This comparison shows that although there is something in favor of saying a blind man does not fully understand the meaning of color words, there is no parallel feature in favor of saying that Robinson does not understand the meaning of "pain." The comparison supports the view that congenital incapacity to feel pain does not logically imply any failure to understand the word, or to "know what pain is."

The phrase "understanding a concept" is a philosopher's expression, and its meaning tends to be nebulous. I am suggesting that we explicate this notion in terms of *abilities*—that is, what a man *can do*. Taking the notion in this light, we see that Robinson's full repertoire of abilities to use the word "pain" correctly implies a full understanding of the *concept* of pain.

### 16. Ostensive Definition Revisited

The chief source of the inclination to assume that a person who had never felt pain could not know the meaning of the word is the thought that it would be impossible for him to give himself an *ostensive definition* of pain. Therefore he would never know to *what* the word "pain" *refers*. He might be skillful at imitating the behavior of a person in pain; he could be very good at discerning whether others were in pain (by observation of their circumstances and behavior); somehow or other he might even be distressed by the sufferings of others; but still he would not know *what* pain is. He would not have experienced a direct awareness of pain. Thus he could not have connected the word "pain" *with pain itself.* The most he could understand the word to mean would be certain *behavior* in certain *circumstances.*

This view is related to a problem about the nature of naming. Philosophers have often assumed that you can give an object a name, without knowing or implying anything whatever about the properties of the object. The name would have "denotation without connotation." J. S. Mill held that all *proper* names serve as names in this way. He says that "whenever the names given to objects convey any information, that is, whenever they have properly any meaning, the meaning resides not in what they *denote,* but in what they *connote.* The only names of objects which connote nothing are *proper* names. . . ." [52] "A proper name is but an unmeaning mark which we connect in our minds with the idea of the object, in order that whenever the mark meets our eyes or occurs to our thoughts, we may think of that individual object."[53]

Mill's doctrine is intended to hold only for *proper* names, not for *general* names. Nevertheless it helps to provide a picture of how the ostensive definition of pain is to be conceived. Each of us is to say to himself, *"This* is *pain,"* while he fixes his attention on "a certain sensation." This "ceremony" (as Wittgenstein calls it) is supposed to enable us to apply the name "pain" to that same sensation when

52. J. S. Mill, *A System of Logic,* 8th ed., new impression (London, 1949), Bk. I, Ch. 2, Sec. 5.
53. *Ibid.*

it occurs in us again. The ostensive definition must be inward and private. For each of us it provides the word "pain" with a direct reference to pain itself, not merely to its manifestations or causes or consequences in behavior. We can perform in our minds the act of connecting the word with the sensation without having any information *about* the sensation. Russell's famous distinction between "knowledge by acquaintance" and "knowledge by description" can be applied here. The former is "logically independent of knowledge of truths," whereas the latter involves some knowledge of truths. Russell illustrates this distinction by reference to the color of a table:

> The particular shade of colour that I am seeing may have many things said about it—I may say that it is brown, that it is rather dark, and so on. But such statements, though they make me know truths *about* the colour, do not make me know the colour itself any better than I did before: so far as concerns knowledge of the colour itself, as opposed to knowledge of truths about it, I know the colour perfectly and completely when I see it, and no further knowledge of it itself is even theoretically possible.[54]

What Russell said here about color he would also have said about pain, and all other "sense-data." Our ostensive definition will enable us to know pain itself, even in the absence of any previous knowledge about it.

54. Bertrand Russell, *The Problems of Philosophy* (New York, 1912), pp. 72–74.

But decisive objections now arise to oppose the idea that inner ostensive definition can achieve *anything*:

(1) There is the insoluble problem as to how my own ostensive definition could teach me what the word "pain" denotes. For this is a word in the English language, a word used by many people. If I know only from my own case what the denotation of the word is, then I know only what *I* call "pain," not what anyone else does.[55] If each of us gave himself an inner definition this could not provide for a *common* use of the word. The inner, private object might be *different* in each case. If it were the same this could not be known. Our inclination to believe that Robinson, the pain-less man, cannot know *what* the word "pain" means, assumes that the word has an agreed-on application. His inability to give himself an ostensive definition of pain (or at least the right one) was supposed to prevent him from bestowing on his use of the word this *common* reference. By implication, the common reference is supposed to be produced by a multitude of individual, private, ostensive definitions. But this could not be so. A host of private objects could contribute no more than a single one could to a use of language on which people *agreed*.[56] If Robinson were to have pain for the first time and were to define it ostensively as "pain," this could not help him to know what the English word "pain" means. Nor could it help others to know

---

55. Wittgenstein, *Investigations*, Sec. 347.
56. Cf. *ibid.*, Sec. 293.

what he meant. The inward pointing would be useless.

(2) If I gave myself an inner ostensive definition of pain, this would be supposed to bring about the result that in the future I should continue to call the same inner occurrence "pain." But will it mean anything to pick out the *same* occurrence? Could I go wrong? What would be the difference between going right and going wrong?

It would be no answer to say that in the one case I should be calling *the same thing* "pain" and in the other case, not. As Peter Geach remarks, " 'The same' is a fragmentary expression, and has no significance unless we say or mean 'the same *X*,' where '*X*' represents a general term . . ." such as *man,* or *river,* or *sensation:* "there is no such thing as being just 'the same.' "[57] But as we saw previously, I can have no justification for saying that what I picked out and labeled with the word "pain" was *pain.* It might have been something else—perhaps just an inward groan. I am not even entitled to say it was a *sensation.*[58] All I can say is that it was "the same" (which means as much and as little as "the same *X*" or "the same *thing*") without being able to specify any general term. If you say "I have the same again," you will not be expressing a complete thought (unless the context supplies the general

57. Peter Geach, *Mental Acts* (London, 1957), p. 69. See also John Cook, "Wittgenstein on Privacy," *Philosophical Review*, Vol. 74, No. 3, July 1965, p. 305.
58. Wittgenstein, *Investigations*, Sec. 261.

term). It would be like saying "I am as tall as." If
we complete the thought by inserting a general term
after "the same" (such as *disease* or *sensation* or
*pain*), then that general term brings in *criteria of
identity*. The criteria differ with each general term.
The criteria of identity for *rivers* are not the same
as for *hurricanes*. The criteria of identity for
*thoughts* are different from those for *sensations*. If
I say that *A* and *B* are the same *X*, the "*X*" is a
mere blank that must be filled in with a general term
that is either specified or understood from the context of discourse. The general term will carry criteria
of identity with it, in terms of which my judgment of
identity will be right or wrong. If I will not bring in
a general term, but merely assert that *A* and *B* are
the *same,* there will be *no* right or wrong in what
I say.

Such would be the predicament of anyone who
tried to acquire through introspection any "simple
ideas of reflection." We have concentrated on the
overworked example of *pain* because there is little
inclination to regard it as analyzable into other concepts,[59] and also because pains are genuinely objects
of attention, not "dissolving" when Wittgenstein's
technique of description is brought to bear. It would
seem that there could not be a more perfect example
of a simple concept obtained from introspection. Yet
we see that the inner ostensive definition cannot bear
the burden placed on it. There can be no warrant for

---

59. Although Russell did regard it so in *The Analysis of Mind.*

asserting that (even probably) the something on which I concentrated my attention and labeled "pain" was *pain*. The inner definition cannot be claimed to provide me with a knowledge of *what pain is*—which is why it was thought to be necessary in the first place. Furthermore, it cannot be specified *at all* what the thing is that I am supposed to have named. This has the consequence that it will be *meaningless* to say that I have gone on, in the future, to apply the word "pain" to the *same* thing, in agreement with the definition. The "ceremony" that was felt to be all-important has turned out to be completely empty.

## 17. Getting Rid of the Private Object

Wittgenstein makes this startling remark: "You learned the *concept* 'pain' when you learned language."[60] Why is it startling? Because it seems to ignore what is most important, namely, one's experience of pain itself. One wants to exclaim: "You have not learned the *concept* until you have learned *what* pain is, and this requires the experience of pain. In learning language you might come to know a lot about how to *use* the *word:* but this will not give you the essential thing." Here we are pleading the necessity of an inner exhibition. But what we should now admit, no matter how contrary to our philosophical inclinations, is that the inner exhibition can con-

60. Wittgenstein, *Investigations*, Sec. 384.

tribute nothing to the understanding of a concept. It can have no significant consequences. Our observation of what goes on in our own minds cannot be a requirement for our learning of *any* concept, whether of "tangible" or "intangible" mental phenomena.

The bearing of these remarks on our example of Robinson, who has never felt pain, is clear enough. The range of abilities we attributed to him was adequate to characterize him as having a full understanding of the concept of pain. Our inclination to insist that it was not enough is due to our picture of Robinson's being required to address the words *"this* is pain" to an inner something. But the question arises as to *what* this inner object is, or whether it is *anything:* and also whether Robinson's application of the word "pain," on subsequent occasions, is to the *same* object or to a different one.

Wittgenstein employs the trick of imagining someone with a very bad memory:

> "Imagine a person whose memory could not retain *what* the word 'pain' meant—so that he constantly called different things by that name—but nevertheless used the word in a way fitting in with the usual symptoms and presuppositions of pain"—in short he uses it as we all do. Here I should like to say: a wheel that can be turned though nothing else moves with it, is not part of the mechanism.[61]

Wittgenstein also supplies this piece of tactical advice: "Always get rid of the idea of the private object in this way: assume that it constantly changes,

61. *Ibid.*, Sec. 271.

but that you do not notice the change because your memory constantly deceives you.''[62]

The hypothesis of a bad memory is not to be taken with a straight face. It is a philosophical joke. Since (on the assumption of a private definition) the supposition that I do or do not apply the name ''pain'' to the *same* inner thing is meaningless, it is equally meaningless to suppose that my *memory* of doing the same is correct or that it is incorrect. If we are inclined to take quite seriously the assumption that I must apply the word ''pain'' to something which only I *can* know, then the point of Wittgenstein's trick is to make us realize that I could not defend, as correct, my recollection of having done the *right* thing. Indeed, there would be *no* difference between my remembering and my seeming to myself to remember. We are helped to see that the very notion of my ''doing the right thing'' will be a sham. My ''memory'' of it would be neither correct nor incorrect, because there would be nothing that *made* the memory true or false. There would be nothing for the memory to be true *to*.

Someone uses the word ''pain'' correctly, or he does not. This can be determined. We do not know how to make a distinction between his being able to *use* the word correctly and his *knowing its meaning*. Our attempt to make such a distinction, by appealing to an inner ostensive definition, is a failure.

62. *Ibid.*, p. 207.

No concepts whatever can be obtained, even partly, from Locke's "reflection." We must reject the doctrine, so powerful in modern philosophy, that we acquire concepts of mental occurrences by observing those occurrences taking place in ourselves. In rejecting it we remove the chief source of the temptation to think that a human mind could exist and be provided with concepts, in isolation from a human body and from a community of living human beings.

# II.

# *Materialism*

———◆◆◆◆———

## 18.  Minds and Brains

Many philosophers have been unable to stomach an ultimate dualism of mind and matter, and have been drawn to various forms of monism. One of these is an idealistic monism which holds that sensations, perceptions, and mental processes in general comprise "the ultimate furniture of the world." In one version of idealism, material bodies and physical processes are illusory appearances. In another version matter is not an illusion but is made up of the mental; bodies are "bundles of sensations"; the physical world is "constructed" by us out of mental experience. Another form of monism professes to be "neutral" as between mind and matter. There is a neutral stuff called "pure experience" or "the instant field of the present" (William James), which in certain relationships constitutes the "objective" or physical and in other relationships comprises the "subjective" or mental. This view is obscure and will not be studied in this essay. A third form of monism is materialism. The most plausible and cogent variety of materialism is logical behaviorism. According to it the existence of mental states and processes is not denied, but they are thought of as logical constructions out of the movements, utterances, and dispositions of the human body. This view will be studied in Part III of the present essay.

We shall be concerned now with another form of materialism which is currently attracting interest. This materialism is appropriately called "scientific" because it holds that everything in the world consists, "in the last resort," of "the ultimate entities of physics,"[63] and is ultimately governed by the laws of physics. There are no nonphysical entities or nonphysical laws. Men and animals are complicated physical mechanisms.

A philosopher holding this position may combine it with behaviorism. Or he may go only part of the way with behaviorism. J. J. C. Smart is a leading exponent of this latter position. He thinks there is plausibility in regarding vanity, anger, or fear as mere "behavior patterns." But he also thinks there are "inner experiences" that cannot plausibly be analyzed in terms of behavior. It is not surprising that Smart's examples of such "inner experiences" are taken from the class of "tangible" mental phenomena to which we referred in Part I—for example, sensations and images. Smart says:

63. J. J. C. Smart, "Materialism," *Journal of Philosophy*, Vol. 60, No. 22, October 1963, p. 651.

Suppose that I report that I am having an orange-yellow roundish after-image. Or suppose again that I report that I have a pain. It seems clear that the content of my report cannot be exclusively a set of purely behavioural facts. There seems to be some element of "pure inner experience" which is being reported, and to which only I have direct access.[64]

These experiences are kept within the scheme of materialism by holding that they are *brain processes*. There is a subtlety in this view which must be noted. Although Smart sometimes expresses himself as asserting that experiences *are* brain processes, sometimes he states his view to be that they *may be* brain processes: "it may be the true nature of our inner experiences, as revealed by science, to be brain processes."[65] Smart's position is that *if* the experience of feeling pain or of having an afterimage is a brain process, this is only *contingently* so. It could have been otherwise, and indeed may be otherwise. His main concern is to establish that it is a *possibility*, as a conceptual matter, that experiences are brain processes; that scientific research *might* prove it to be so; that it cannot be ruled out *a priori*. Smart is happy to concede that "when I say 'I have a yellowish-orange after-image' I cannot *mean* that I have such-and-such brain process."[66] If there is an identity between "inner experiences" and brain processes, it must be conceived of as purely contingent, not as logically necessary.

64. Smart, *Philosophy and Scientific Realism* (New York, 1963), p. 89.

65. *Ibid.*, p. 93.

66. *Ibid.*, pp. 93–94.

This negative aspect of Smart's materialism has merit even if the affirmative aspect does not. It is true that our concepts of the mental (thinking, sensation, intention, emotion, feeling, et cetera), as they are employed in ordinary life and language, are not tied to any concepts of inner physiological processes, whether of brain, stomach, or liver. We know that our daughter is afraid of the neighbor's shaggy dog, but we do not know anything about the condition of her brain. We know that our dinner companion just this moment decided to order beef instead of fish, but we know nothing, and care nothing, about what physical processes may be going on inside his skull. As youngsters we learn to use the verbs of sensation, cognition, or intention, without having any knowledge, or even any beliefs, about the inner physiology of human beings. We say we know our friend is crying from pain, because we saw him crack his shin on the porch step. But if we were asked whether we are sure that such-and-such a process is taking place in his brain, we should not understand the relevance of the question: it would be an irritating change of subject. Our common procedures of *verifying* that someone feels cold, sees an afterimage, heard the warning gun, suddenly recognized a face in the crowd, are not connected with investigations of inner physiology.

In the light of these facts it is a matter of some curiousness that when people begin their first philosophizing about mind, they have a considerable propensity to *identify* mind as brain. A college undergraduate, in his first course in philosophy, will speak quite spontaneously of some thought, or visual impression, as *taking place in his brain,* and at the same time he will *point to his head.* It is also curious that in ordinary language such idioms as "He has a good brain" and "He has a good mind" are used almost interchangeably (mainly with the meaning that the person in question is intelligent). A possible guess would be that the naturalness of the brain-idioms, and of the primitive philosophical tendency, is due to such facts as that the organs of sight, smell, and hearing are located in the head (that is, we see, hear, and smell *from the head*); and that when we are engaged in hard thinking we tend to press our brows and scratch our heads; and also that as we concentrate we are often aware of sensations of muscular strain in the vicinity of the eyes and ears. In contrast, there is no natural tendency to locate emotions, such as fear or rage, in the head, but rather in the breast. This might be partly due to the alterations of breathing and heartbeat in emotion, and to our tendency to clutch our breasts in fear, to swell with rage, and so on.

Leaving aside these natural propensities, and how to explain them, it is obvious that the mastery all of us acquire of our ordinary discourse about mental occurrences and states is not based on the acquisition of knowledge of brain processes. It is an understatement to say that we should not count it a failure in someone to understand the meaning of the words "thinking" or "seeing" if he did not believe that thinking and seeing occur inside our skulls. Smart is right not to permit the putative identity of mental events with brain events to be guaranteed on conceptual grounds.

## 19. Contingent Identity

If the claimed identity between a thought or sensation or state of consciousness and some process in the brain is understood to be contingent, then it should be capable of being proved or disproved by *empirical* investigation. Is this a possibility? It should be noted that Smart's view is not that there is merely a *correlation* between a certain mental event and a certain brain event. Even a systematic correlation or a causal relationship would not suffice. For this would imply that the mental event and the correlated brain event were *two different*, although connected, events. It is Smart's view that empirical investigation might prove that mental events of a certain sort are *"strictly identical"* with brain events of a certain sort.[67] What is supposed to be capable of being proved is that some one and the same event should be both a sudden thought, or a feeling of pain, and also an event inside the skull.

If Smart's phrase "strict identity" is going to have any meaning over and above systematic and/or causal connection, then it should be subject to the following necessary condition: If $x$ occurs in a cer-

67. Smart, "Sensations and Brain Processes," *Philosophical Review*, Vol. 68, 1959; reprinted in *Body and Mind*, ed. G. N. A. Vesey (London, 1964), see pp. 427–428.

tain place at a certain time, then *y* is strictly identical with *x only* if *y* occurs in the same place at the same time. [68] Smart thinks that a flash of lightning, for example, is "strictly identical" with an electric discharge. But he would not believe this if he did not think that when a flash of lightning occurs, an electrical discharge occurs at the same time and in the same place.

U. T. Place is another writer who expounds the same materialist position. An example that he uses to illustrate the sense of "identity" in which, according to him, "consciousness" could turn out to be identical with brain processes is the following: "A cloud is a mass of water droplets or other particles in suspension."[69] It is pretty obvious that Place would not hold this to be an example of identity, *as contrasted with* systematic and/or causal correlation, if he did not assume that in the region of space occupied by a cloud there is, at the same time, a mass of particles in suspension.

It will be evident upon reflection that the stated necessary condition for identity (as contrasted with correlation) cannot be satisfied if *x* is a brain process and *y* is, for example, a sudden thought or a feeling of pain. A brain process occurs at a certain time in a certain location. It will be an electrical, mechanical,

68. Cf. my article "Scientific Materialism and the Identity Theory," *Dialogue*, Vol. 3, No. 2, 1964, pp. 116–119.

69. U. T. Place, "Is Consciousness A Brain Process?" *British Journal of Psychology*, Vol. 47, 1956; reprinted in *The Philosophy of Mind*, ed. V. C. Chappell (Englewood Cliffs, N.J., 1962), pp. 103–105.

chemical, or some other sort of physical occurrence inside the skull. Such an occurrence could be verified by means of scientific instruments. It could also be verified that this occurrence took place at the exact time that the person whose skull it was had a sudden thought or felt a stab of pain. But a further requirement for the claimed *identity* would be that the person's sudden thought had occurred *inside his skull*. Could this be determined?

It should be noted that since the identity is presumed to be *contingent*, the method of determining that a *thought* or *thinking* was located inside the skull would have to be *logically independent* of the method of determining the occurrence of the correlated brain process. Employing the occurrence of the brain process as the *criterion* of the occurrence of the thought inside the skull would prevent the putative identity from having an empirical verification. It would no longer be conceived of as a contingent identity. There would be a connection of *meaning* between saying that a certain brain process occurred inside someone's skull and saying that a certain thought occurred in the same place.

In order to keep the alleged identity purely contingent, and its verification purely empirical, one would need to have a procedure of verifying the occurrence of a thought inside the skull which was *not* conceived of as consisting in the verification of the occurrence of some physical process inside the skull. Presumably scientific instruments would be employed.

We can see that the undertaking would be unintelligible. No kind of observation, or of investigation with instruments, could determine the presence of thinking inside the skull, *unless* the investigation was conceived of as determining the occurrence of some physical process inside the skull, the occurrence of which was itself to be used as the criterion of the occurrence of thinking inside the skull. But if the investigation was so conceived the identity would not be contingent.

We are able to determine that a person had a certain thought at a certain time by perceiving some expression of the thought in utterance or action. And this *is* conceptually independent of the investigation of brain processes. But this way of determining the occurrence of a thought tells us nothing about *a bodily location* of the thought. We do not understand what the bodily location of a thought, or of thinking, would mean. Jerome Shaffer puts the point as follows:

> The physical events which are intimately connected with my having particular mental events have some definite location, probably in the brain. This is not to say that they are localized in some small part of the brain or even in a number of small parts of the brain. Perhaps they are spread throughout large parts of the brain; perhaps they are fields; perhaps they include the nonoccurrence of certain events. Nevertheless such phenomena occur not only at some time but also in some place or places in the brain. However, so far as thoughts are concerned, it makes no sense to talk about a thought's being located in some place or places in the body. If I report having suddenly thought something,

the question *where* in my body that thought occurred would be utterly senseless. It would be as absurd to wonder whether that thought had occurred in my foot, throat, or earlobe as it would be to wonder whether that thought might have been cubical or a micron in diameter.[70]

Since the notion of a bodily location of thinking does not have any meaning at present, it *can* have meaning only if it is *given* meaning. One way this could come about would be through adopting the convention that the occurrence of a certain physiological process in a certain place (for example, the brain) would signify the occurrence of thinking in that place. This would be a definition of what the latter meant. But the identity of thinking and physiological process, which would emerge from this convention, would not be a contingent identity. It would have been "verified," in part, by legislating sense into an expression that presently does not have sense.

If we turn from thinking to bodily sensations the matter is different, since aches, twinges, et cetera, do have bodily locations. They are located on the skin, or in a tooth or limb, but never in the brain. Bodily sensations are located where they are *felt* to be.[71] People do not feel sensations in their brains. (Brain tissue

70. J. A. Shaffer, "Recent Work on the Mind-Body Problem," *American Philosophical Quarterly*, Vol. 2, No. 2, 1965, p. 97. See also my "Scientific Materialism and the Identity Theory," *op. cit.*, pp. 119–120.
71. See my article "The Privacy of Experience," *Theory of Knowledge*, ed. Avrum Stroll (New York, 1966).

is actually insensitive.) Therefore, bodily sensations are not brain processes.

Smart makes a remark about afterimages which could be applied to bodily sensations. He says his view is not that *an afterimage* is a brain process, but that *the experience of having* an afterimage is a brain process.[72] He might wish to say, similarly, that the having or the experience of having a sensation is a brain process, not that the sensation is. In this way he would avoid the absurdly false result that all bodily sensations are located in or on the brain.

But Smart would avoid the false only by incurring the meaningless. For the case stands with *the having* or *the experience* of having a sensation, just as it stands with thoughts and thinking. It has no meaning to ask for the bodily location of *an experience,* or of *the having* of a sensation. It could acquire meaning only through a new convention.

Smart's general position can be seen to be hopeless. It is logically impossible that the claimed contingent identity of mental events with brain processes could be proved or disproved empirically. It is not a possible scientific hypothesis. Thoughts, "inner experiences,"states of consciousness, could not turn out to be nor not to be brain events or brain states. The conjecture that the two kinds of phenomena might prove to be contingently identical is not false but meaningless.

72. Smart, "Sensations and Brain Processes," *Body and Mind,* ed. Vesey, p. 432.

## 20. Conceptual Revision

Smart has taken notice of the criticism that, as he puts it, "ordinary language implies that conscious experiences are not in physical space" and therefore "it is contrary to ordinary language to say that conscious experiences are brain processes."[73] He replies as follows:

> I am not sure how one decides between the hypothesis (a) that ordinary language ascribes *no* place to conscious states and (b) that it simply *leaves open* what place they are in, or indeed whether they are in any place at all. If, however, hypothesis (a) is accepted, then it must be admitted that I have not perfectly reconciled the brain process theory with ordinary language. To some extent ordinary language would have to be said to embody a dualistic metaphysics. Nevertheless, the switch in ordinary language to bring it in line with hypothesis (b) would be a very simple and painless one, involving hardly any readjustments to the rest of language.[74]

Smart thinks that *if* it would be a "conceptual revision" to locate "conscious experiences" in the head, it would be a revision that was reasonable "in the light of present scientific knowledge."[75]

These remarks show a failure to feel the weight of his predicament. Changes in concepts (that is, in

73. Smart, *Philosophy and Scientific Realism*, p. 98.
74. *Ibid.*
75. *Ibid.*

the use of expressions) certainly do occur. At one
time the attributing of *numerical values* to tempera-
tures had no meaning; but the invention and use of
the thermometer provided a meaning for it. If systematic correlations were discovered to hold between
sudden thoughts and certain brain events, it is possible that the occurrence of the right sort of brain
event would, in certain circumstances, come to be
used as a criterion of the occurrence of the correlated
thought. It could even happen that the thought came
to be spoken of as occurring *where* the brain event
had occurred. We should then have a definition of the
"location" of a thought. You could tell someone
what it meant. Just as you can explain what it means
to say that the lake is "three degrees warmer" today
than yesterday.

But if a "revision" or "readjustment", no matter
how reasonable, simple and painless, would be
necessary in order to give any *sense* to the conjecture
that mental events are identical with brain events,
then *as things stand with our concepts* this conjecture cannot admit of empirical proof or disproof. By
readjusting our language we could "prove" many
wonderful things—for example, that tables lay eggs,
or that eggs lay tables. Smart's confession that because of the alleged bias of ordinary language towards "a dualistic metaphysics," some revision of
language is required in order to establish the identity
conjecture as true is an admission that it is not a
logical possibility that the conjecture should be es-
tablished as contingently true or as contingently
false.

## 21. The Brain as the Subject of Experience

Smart thinks not only that it could turn out that thoughts and experiences are brain processes, but also that *the brain* has thoughts and experiences. He says:

> In some future state of physiological technology we might be able to keep a human brain alive *in vitro.* Leaving the question of the morality of such an experiment to one side, let us suppose that the experiment is done. By suitable electrodes inserted into appropriate parts of this brain we get it to have the illusion of perceiving things and also to have pains, and feelings of moving its nonexistent limbs, and so on. (This brain might even be able to think verbally, for it might have learned a language before it was put *in vitro,* or else, by suitable signals from our electrodes, we might even give it the illusion of learning a language in the normal way.)[76]

Smart believes that the possibility of the described experiment proves that the human body and human behavior are not "essential" or "important" for the existence of "mental experiences." He remarks that "what is important in psychology is what goes on in the central nervous system, not what goes on in the face, larynx, and limbs."[77] The examples of the brain *in vitro* shows that what is essential to a pain is what goes on in the brain, not what goes on in the arms or legs or larynx or mouth."[78]

76. Smart, "Materialism," *op. cit.*, p. 659.
77. *Ibid.*
78. *Ibid.*, p. 660.

We must disentangle two theses in Smart's remarks. One is that the brain is essential, and the rest
of the human body not essential, for the occurrence
of mental events. The other is that the brain itself
is (or might turn out to be) that which thinks, feels
and has sensations. Let us turn to the imagined experiment. We shall assume that it is known that
certain brain processes occur when and only when
certain mental events occur. The brain of a human
person (call him Hansen) has been separated from
the rest of his body and kept alive. It is discovered
that there occurs in the isolated brain some process,
*P*, known to be uniquely correlated with (let us suppose) the hearing of a buzzing sound. Should we
conclude that Hansen hears a buzzing sound? No; for
Hansen is dead. His body, except for the brain, is
moldering away. Should we conclude that the isolated brain hears a buzzing sound? No. Our original
datum was that *people* hear buzzing sounds if and
only if *P* occurs in their brains. Nothing was determined about the conditions under which *brains* hear
buzzing sounds. The experiment would have shown
that *P* can occur, in an isolated brain, when *no*
buzzing sound is heard. The experiment would have
done nothing to confirm either of Smart's theses.

We can imagine still other experiments. Suppose
that Hansen's brain was removed and not kept alive,
but that after the operation Hansen continued to
live as a normal person—to walk and talk, to express thoughts and sensations, and to hear buzzing
sounds. This experiment would show that the brain

is not necessary for normal mental life, and the logical possibility of such an outcome shows that the brain is not *logically* necessary for normal mental life. Our previous remarks (Section 18) about the *non*connectedness of the concepts of the mental with the concepts of inner physiology will help to make this assertion plausible.

Thus Smart's contention that brain events are essential for mental life, and "bodily behavior" is not, is the exact reverse of the truth. Our concepts of the mental are heavily based on the human form, and on facial expression and bodily movement, but not at all on happenings in the central nervous system. Whether our friend's face is calm or angry, whether he started and gasped or sat relaxed and smiling—such facts have an important bearing on what he thought or felt or saw, not merely on the verification of it but on the meaning of it. You could not explain to someone the concepts of decision, doubt, pain, or anger by referring him to cerebral processes. You can make a start on it by giving him *examples*. In doing this you would be drawing attention to the postures, movements, changes of countenance, actions, and utterances of living human beings, and you would also be showing the connection between this behavior and the various circumstances that provide an *occasion* for anger or a *setting* for doubt or decision.

Let us imagine still another experiment. We shall suppose that whenever a man's brain is in his skull, and is artificially stimulated in a specific area, he will regularly report a certain experience. Now we shall suppose that (a) Hansen's brain is removed from his skull and that both his brain and his body are kept alive, although his body is inert and insensitive; (b) Hansen's brain is artificially stimulated in the specified area; (c) Hansen's brain is then restored to his body; (d) on recovering consciousness, Hansen reports that he remembers experiences such as *would have* resulted from that stimulation when his brain was in his body.[79] Would these facts, all of which are conceivable, be evidence that Hansen's isolated *brain* had those experiences? Or would it be evidence that *Hansen* had those experiences when his brain and body were separated?

First of all, we are not required to assume that anyone or anything had experiences. The experiment could be taken as a proof that the stimulation of the isolated brain, and its later restoration, caused Hansen to have the *delusion* of seeming to recall experiences that, in fact, did not occur. In order to produce a clear case for Hansen's having a certain experience during the period of separation, as contrasted with his having a subsequent delusion of memory, we should need to alter the imagined facts. The original supposition was that during the period of separation Hansen remained alive (his breathing and heartbeat were maintained), yet he was inert and totally unresponsive to stimulation. These facts would require us to say that Hansen was *unconscious* during the period of separation. This excludes the supposi-

79. I owe this example to Peter Geach.

tion that he had some experience or other during that period. (If one thinks that Hansen might have had a certain experience while *unconscious,* what would distinguish this from the supposition that he did *not* have the experience but merely had the subsequent false impression of having had it?)

Second, these facts could not be evidence that the isolated *brain* had experiences. Everything said in Sections 8 and 9 about the senselessness of attributing experiences to stones or chairs, holds equally true for brains. No experiment could establish that a brain thinks or feels because a brain does not sufficiently resemble a human being.[80] *People* see, hear, think—not brains. A person can *look* attentive, surprised, or frightened (and so can a dog); but a brain cannot. Not only cannot a brain *display* interest or anger, but it could not have *objects of interest* or *occasions for anger.* It could not engage in any of the activities that are required for the application of those concepts. A brain does not have the right physiognomy nor the capacity for participating in any of the forms of life that would be required for it to be a subject of experience.

## 22. Direct and Private Access

It is of some interest to speculate on the causes of the inclination to think that mental events could be proved to be brain processes. One factor is a revolt against Cartesian dualism. Another factor is a belief

80. Cf. Wittgenstein, *Investigations,* Secs. 281, 283.

in scientific materialism. These two, however, could more easily result in some form of behaviorism. A third factor is the feeling that there are mental phenomena which will not yield to behavioristic reduction, because they are intractably "inner." Smart says about his report of a pain: "It seems clear that the content of my report cannot be exclusively a set of purely behavioural facts. There seems to be some element of 'pure inner experience' which is being reported, and to which only I have direct access."[81] A fourth factor is the common knowledge that the brain stands in a unique causal relationship to many sensations and mental events. A fifth factor, probably, is the fact that we perceive the world, by sight, hearing, and smell, "from our heads" (Section 18).

The third factor in this diagnosis is of particular interest, because it is this same idea that produces the common philosophical belief in the necessity for private ostensive definitions of the concepts of the mental. This belief tends to generate psychophysical dualism and, finally, solipsism.

It would be punning to say that brain processes and experiences are *both* "inner." This word is used literally in the first case and figuratively in the second. "Experience is inner" is intended to mean something like this: experience is known only to the subject of experience. Or, as Smart puts it, only I have "direct access" to my experience.

Can the notion that the experience of pain is

81. *Philosophy and Scientific Realism*, p. 89.

"inner" be reconciled with the hypothesis that it is a brain process? I am supposed to have "direct access" to my "inner." But I do not even have *access* to my brain processes. Therefore they cannot be that which was presumed to be "inner."

If scientific instruments gave me access to my brain processes, this would not be the *"direct"* access of which Smart spoke. Presumably he was using this word as philosophers normally do, when they speak of "direct knowledge" or "direct awareness" or "direct acquaintance." As they use the word, information or awareness that was based on the use of instruments would not be "direct." Furthermore, the access that instruments gave me to my brain would not be exclusively mine. Others could have the same access.

The upshot is that Smart's theory as to what his experience of having a pain *is* conflicts with his original inclination to think that he is the *only* person who has *direct* access to his own experience. For neither thing would be true if his experience were a brain process. His theory is incompatible with one of the philosophical inclinations that produced it. He could retain the theory and surrender the inclination. But then he would have given up his stated objection to a rival form of materialism, namely, a thorough-going logical behaviorism.[82]

82. *Ibid.*

# III.
# *Logical Behaviorism*

———◆◆◆———

## 23. The Rejection of Introspection

The behaviorism which is the topic here is not a program of experimental inquiry, nor is it the doctrine that "stimulus" and "response" are connected by empirical laws. It is the view that the meaning of mental term such as "thinking," "anger," "intention" can be explained wholly in terms of bodily behavior and of the physical circumstances in which it occurs. As Rudolf Carnap once stated it, it is the thesis that "all sentences of psychology describe physical occurrences, namely the physical behavior of humans and other animals."[83] "Our thesis thus states that a definition may be constructed for every psychological concept (i.e. expression) which directly

---

83. Rudolf Carnap, "Psychology in Physical Language," *Erkenntnis*, Vol. 2, 1931; reprinted in *Logical Positivism*, ed. A. J. Ayer (Glencoe, Ill., 1959), p. 165. Carnap has long since given up logical behaviorism; but this does not diminish the value of his lucid exposition of it.

or indirectly derives that concept from physical concepts."[84] As applied to one's attributions of mental predicates to other persons, the view is that "a singular sentence about other minds always has the same content as some specific physical sentence."[85] "A sentence about other minds states that the body of the person in question is in a physical state of a certain sort."[86] The same analysis holds for one's ascriptions of mental predicates to oneself, "though here the emotional obstacles to a physical interpretation are considerably greater."[87] The contrary view that such sentences about oneself refer to something nonphysical (some "experience-content" or "datum of consciousness") leads to the consequence that those sentences are meaningful only to the person who utters them.[88] In summary, logical behaviorism holds that "so-called psychological sentences—whether they are concrete sentences about other minds, or about some past condition of one's own mind, or about the present condition of one's own mind, or, finally, general sentences—are always translatable into physical language," that is, into sentences about physical occurrences and physical states.[89]

This doctrine is a natural opponent of the Lockean view that mental concepts are obtained from intro-

84. *Ibid.*, p. 167.
85. *Ibid.*, p. 175.
86. *Ibid.*
87. *Ibid.*, p. 191.
88. *Ibid.*, p. 192.
89. *Ibid.*, p. 197.

spection. The behaviorist philosophers have realized
that the absolute divorcing of mental concepts from
observable behavior must lead to solipsism.[90] In the
present essay the further point has been made that
the assumption that one's mental concepts are derived from "one's own case," leads to meaningless-
ness even in one's own case.[91]

Although logical behaviorism correctly rejects the
Lockean theory of the introspective origin of mental
concepts, it is mistaken in other respects. The ex-
planation of what is wrong with it is one of the most
challenging problems of philosophy. In the following sections two fundamental criticisms of logical behaviorism will be proposed.


## 24. The Asymmetry in Mental Concepts

The most persuasive part of behaviorism is its account of the meaning of one's sentences about the
thoughts and feelings of persons other than oneself.
My statement to someone that Robinson feels ill
certainly is supported or refuted by Robinson's
demeanor, actions, and utterances. If I failed to
realize that this was the method of verification, it
would be a failure to understand the *meaning* of such
a statement. The insight (elaborated in Part I) that
inner ostensive definition and the private object can

90. See Section 8 above. Cf. my "Behaviorism as a Philosophy of
Psychology," *Behaviorism and Phenomenology*, ed. T. W. Wann
(Chicago, 1964), pp. 148–149.
91. Section 16 above.

play no part in our understanding of statements about other minds, and therefore that this understanding cannot be founded on an analogy with one's own case, *seems* to force us to the conclusion that the meaning of those statements is entirely exhausted by their reference to observable behavior.

Behaviorist philosophers made the natural assumption that ascriptions of mental predicates to oneself and to other persons would be symmetrical in respect of verification. Carnap thought that my statement "I am excited" obtains its "rational support" from observations such as would be expressed by the sentences "I see my hands trembling," "I hear my voice quavering," and so on.[92] But reflection on the use of these sentences reveals that this is not so. If you did not believe that I am excited, I might try to convince *you* by making you take note of how my hands are trembling. But I do not undertake to convince myself that I am excited by such an observation; or if I did, it would be a very untypical case. If I say "I am annoyed with her because of her refusal to meet us," my statement will not normally be based on my observation of my own physical expressions of annoyance. Nor do I say I am angry because I see that my face is flushed or my fist are clenched, or because I hear myself shouting. In the normal case I do not say it on the basis of the observation of *anything*.

There is a vexing problem here, namely, how can

92. Carnap, *op. cit.*, p. 191.

we *learn* to apply to *ourselves* the language of mental terms? How do I learn when to say the words, "I am annoyed with her" or "I intend to leave at ten-thirty"? The behaviorist B. F. Skinner has expressed some perplexity about this matter. A speaker's statements about his own intentions "describe states of affairs which appear to be accessible only to the speaker. How can the verbal community establish responses of this sort?"[93] Skinner's conjecture is that, first, a person is taught to use this language when he is exhibiting the right public behavior. Then internal physical variables (called "private stimuli") come to be associated with the "public manifestations." Subsequently the person responds to these "private stimuli" when they occur without the public manifestations. The sentence "I was on the point of going home," Skinner suggests, "may be regarded as the equivalent of 'I observed events in myself which characteristically precede or accompany my going home.' "[94]

In fact, however, people do not base their announcements of their intentions on their awareness of events in their bodies.[95] No one knows what these internal physical occurrences would be which are supposed to "characteristically" precede or accompany my going home, signing my name, making a phone call, or any of the innumerable actions which I

93. B. F. Skinner, *Science and Human Behavior* (New York, 1953), p. 262.

94. *Ibid.*

95. Cf. my "Behaviorism as a Philosophy of Psychology," *op. cit.*, pp. 151–152 (see footnote 90 above).

can announce myself as about to do. Skinner's conjecture is wildly remote from the facts. It is a
theoretical solution of a problem which is generated
solely by the false assumption that a speaker's true
statements about what he intends, thinks, or wants,
must be based on the speaker's *observation of something*.

It is an understatement to say that I *do not* base
my statements about my own sensations, thoughts, or
intentions on observation of my bodily movements.
If I *were* to do so, no one would understand me. Suppose I say "I am putting on my coat, so plainly I
intend to go home." This remark might be made in
fun. But if I gave the impression of being serious,
others would regard me strangely. If I intend to go
home I should be able to announce this straight off,
without recourse to observation of my behavior. Indeed, if my remark were truly based on such observation of myself, it would not *be* an expression of
*intention*.

I can say of another person, "I know his stomach
hurts from the way he is groaning and doubling
over." But I cannot speak this way of myself, without revealing a ludicrous misunderstanding of the
concept of sensation. I can say of another. person,
"From the look on his face I can tell he is surprised"; but to say this of myself would show that
there is some misunderstanding somewhere.

It is a basic feature of many mental concepts that
there is a radical asymmetry between their application by oneself to oneself, and their application by

oneself to other persons. Mental concepts that are strongly dispositional (for example, love or bravery) do not possess this feature, or at least the asymmetry is not so sharp. But for a great range of mental concepts it is perfectly sharp. I am expected to have evidence for asserting that another person feels ill, or wants to move out of the sun, or intends to leave the house. If I have no evidence, I am not entitled to make those assertions. But in my own case I am not expected, or even permitted, to have *evidence*. It would be improper to say either that I am or that I am not "entitled" to make such statements about my own feelings and intentions. The general point could be put as follows: Many mental concepts are applied by us to other persons on the basis of behavioral criteria, that is, on the basis of some change of countenance, or utterance, or physical action. But we do not apply them to ourselves on this basis. Thus logical behaviorism gives an incorrect account of one part of their use.

A behaviorist might seek to avoid this conclusion by maintaining that utterances such as "I feel ill" or "I am going to leave now" are not really *statements* or *reports* or *descriptions,* and do not have any *cognitive content*. They are exclamations or warnings or signals, whose function is to elicit responses from other persons. They are not counterexamples to the thesis that the cognitive content of psychological sentences can be given a behavioristic analysis.

To this it must be answered that the utterance "I feel ill" can be an exclamation, but also it *can* be a *report*—depending on the circumstances. When you say something about yourself, your utterance might come under many different headings. If you say "I am going to leave now," you might be *expressing resentment* (for the way you have been treated), or you might be *stating your decision* (in the face of threats), or you might be *replying to a question*, or *rejecting temptation*, or *reaffirming a resolution*—to mention a few possibilities. What you are doing by making that utterance is a matter of what had been said before, to whom you are speaking, what the setting is (whether a courtroom trial, a psychological experiment, or a family breakfast).[96] It is simply false that sentences employing mental terms in the first person singular present tense indicative never are used to make statements or reports, or to give descriptions. But when they are so used, the speaker does not normally rely on behavioral criteria. With regard to the claim that these utterances have no "cognitive content," it will have to be said that the meaning of this phrase is too obscure to allow that any recognizably significant assertion has been made.

## 25. The Asymmetry as Implying Two Senses of Mental Terms

When a philosopher perceives the difference in the application of mental terms by oneself to others and by oneself to oneself, he may again feel the threat

96. Cf. Wittgenstein, *Investigations*, pp. 187–188.

of solipsism. He may think as follows: "In applying these terms to others one must learn to use behavioral criteria; in applying them to oneself one must learn *not* to use behavioral criteria. In one case the meaning of one's statements is connected with behavior; in the other case, not. One cannot be saying the same *kind* of thing in the two cases. In their application to other persons one's statements must be, essentially, about the behavior of bodies. But when applying mental terms to oneself, one cannot be referring to behavior. Therefore one cannot mean that another person is angry in the same sense that oneself is. In the latter case 'anger' means *anger itself;* in the other case it means *behavior*."

But it is not true that I have two concepts of pain, one that I apply to myself and one that I apply to you. The two kinds of application I make of the term "pain," to myself (without criteria) and to you (with criteria), are not isolated from one another. This can be seen from the fact that someone's failure to master *either* kind of application would lead us to say that he does not understand the word. We should not trust his "testimony" that he feels pain if his judgments that others feel pain wildly disregarded the appropriate criteria. Similarly, if he attributed pain to himself on the basis of his own behavior, we should think he had some strange misconception of what the word means, even if his judgments about others were accurate and based on the normal criteria.

Furthermore, it is far from true that the application of mental terms to myself, by myself, is unconnected with my behavior. As Wittgenstein remarks, I do not say that I am in pain, or that I am talking to myself, from observation of my behavior: "But it only makes *sense* because I do behave in this way."[97] Again: "Our criterion for someone's saying something to himself is what he tells us and the rest of his behaviour; and we only say that someone speaks to himself if, in the ordinary sense of the words, he *can speak*. And we do not say it of a parrot; nor of a gramophone."[98]

By virtue of my behavior being thus and so, my elders encouraged me to say that I *want* this, that I *feel dizzy,* that I am *looking at* that object, that I *remember* where I left something, and so on. On the basis of appropriate connections between my behavior and utterances, other persons judged that I had learned to talk. Let us suppose that one day I exclaimed in surprise: "Just now I said some words to myself, not aloud but silently!" My own remark would be used by others as a criterion of my having said something silently to myself. But my remark could be given this weight only because of my previous history of normal human behavior. If this background were taken away, the sounds that came from me would not be speech. This is the meaning of Wittgenstein's aphorism: "If a lion could talk, we could not understand him."[99]

97. *Ibid.,* Sec. 357; italics added.
98. *Ibid.,* Sec. 344.
99. *Ibid.,* p. 223.

There are mental phenomena whose criteria are not linguistic; for example, some forms of pain or fear. Thus we can say that a cat or dog is in pain or afraid. There are many more mental phenomena whose criteria are primarily linguistic. "We say a dog is afraid his master will beat him; but not, he is afraid his master will beat him tomorrow. Why not?"[100] The answer is that the fear of a happening *tomorrow* cannot exist independently of language. It will not make sense to say of a language-less creature that it has this fear, or that it does not have it. Language provides the criterion for the existence of such a fear.

The criteria used by others in applying mental terms to me will sometimes include my nonlinguistic behavior, but sometimes my linguistic behavior—that is, what I say. But the latter can provide criteria only because I have a past history of actions and reactions characteristic of a normal human being.

Psychological sentences in the first person singular present tense indicative are not normally based on criteria; but their second and third person counterparts are. The two categories of statements, although asymmetrical in respect of verification, *cannot* be disconnected in meaning, since there are logical equivalences between them. For example, the statement I should make by saying "I am afraid" would be true if and only if the statement another person would make about me by saying "He is afraid"

100. *Ibid.*, Sec. 650.

would be true. If there were no criteria for the truth or falsity of this third person statement, truth and falsity would have no application to it. But then, neither would they have application to the first person statement, since the first and third person statements have to be logically equivalent in truth value. Thus the possibility of my saying anything true or false by uttering the words "I am afraid" depends upon the existence of behavioral criteria for the truth of the statement "He is afraid." First person utterances and their second and third person counterparts are linked in meaning by virtue of being tied, in different ways, to the same behavioral criteria. This connection prevents it from being true that I have different concepts of pain, or fear, one for myself and one for other persons.

## 26. Attitudes Toward Persons

"My attitude towards him is an attitude towards a soul. I am not of the *opinion* that he has a soul."[101] This remark of Wittgenstein's contains the germ of our second criticism of behaviorism. Let us first develop, by examples, the notion of an "attitude." Wittgenstein calls our attention to a way in which we sometimes regard photographs and pictures. We smile back at the photograph of a smiling friend. Or we feel ourselves rebuked and shamed by the stern gaze that looks out from the picture frame. We may even *speak to* a photograph as if we were speaking

101. Wittgenstein, *Investigations*, p. 178.

to the person himself. We could describe this phenomenon by saying that ''we *regard* the photograph, the picture on our wall, as the object itself (the man, landscape, and so on) depicted there.''[102] We have this attitude more at some times than at others; we do not always feel the gaze from the picture. And we have it more towards some photographs than others.

What is most interesting, however, is to imagine people who did not ever see a photograph of a person *as a person.* Wittgenstein says: ''We could easily imagine people who did not have this relation to such pictures. Who, for example, would be repelled by photographs, because a face without colour and even perhaps a face in reduced proportions struck them as inhuman.''[103]

This example may help to prepare the way for the thought that there is a dimension of our concept of a person which consists of *the way in which we perceive* living human beings. The main problem is whether we can make any sense of the idea that there might be a man whose attitude towards living human beings was no different from his attitude towards any complex physical organism or mechanism.

Let us imagine someone (call him Petersen) who is thoroughly familiar with the ordinary criteria for saying that a human being is angry, or in pain, or believes such-and-such, and so on with the rest of the mental predicates. He can discriminate moods, feelings, thoughts, as well as anyone can. He knows what

102. *Ibid.*, p. 205.
103. *Ibid.* Cf. Sec. 524.

is to be expected from a human being who is resentful, jealous, or depressed. Petersen knows what counts for or against the ascriptions of various mental states to other human beings. Petersen also expresses his own thoughts, desires, sensations, in normal ways. Petersen, as so far described, is like the rest of us. Can something be added to this description that will make it at least doubtful whether Petersen has ''the concept of a person''?

My aim is to try to take logical behaviorism quite seriously by imagining a man who is not merely a theoretical behaviorist but, as we might say, an instinctive or natural behaviorist. He will, in daily life, regard other people in just the way that logical behaviorism implies they should be regarded. What would this be like? According to behaviorism, ''a singular sentence about other minds always has the same content as some specific physical sentence.''[104] It must be remembered that this is a wholly general doctrine. It has the implication that *every* description of human beings, containing mental terms, may be replaced by a *purely physical* description—that is, a description containing no mental terms. As Carnap put it, *''psychology is a branch of physics.''*[105] Physical descriptions are conceived of as the *basic* form of description. From descriptions of physical states and movements one can go, by means of logical constructions, or by means of inferences based on physical laws, to descriptions containing

104. Carnap, *op. cit.*, p. 175.
105. *Ibid.*, p. 197.

mental terms (mental descriptions). One can also go in the other direction, from mental descriptions to physical descriptions, since the relation of translatability is symmetrical. Behaviorism thinks of the physical side of this equivalence as being the more fundamental, and the mental side as derivative.

The viewpoint of logical behaviorism is clearly stated in the following passage:

> The statements of an experimental subject are not, in principle, to be interpreted differently from his other voluntary or involuntary movements—though his speech movements may, under favorable circumstances, be regarded as especially informative. Again, the movements of the speech organs and of the other parts of the body of an experimental subject are not, in principle, to be interpreted differently from the movements of any other animal—though the former may, under favorable circumstances, be more valuable in the construction of general sentences. The movements of an animal are not, again, in principle, to be interpreted any differently from those of a volt-meter—though under favorable circumstances, animal movements may serve scientific purposes in more ways than do the movements of a volt-meter. Finally, the movements of a volt-meter are not, in principle, to be interpreted differently from the movements of a raindrop—though the former offer more opportunities for drawing inferences to other occurrences than do the latter. In all these cases, the issue is basically the same: from a specific physical sentence, other sentences are inferred by a causal argument, i.e. with the help of general physical formulae—the so-called natural laws. The examples cited differ only in the degree of fruitfulness of their premises. Volt-meter readings will, perhaps, justify the inference of a greater number of scientifically important sentences than the behavior of some specific

raindrop will: speech movements will, in a certain respect, justify more such inferences than other human bodily movements will.[106]

Thus a smile, or a look of fear, or a remark or exclamation is not to be "interpreted" differently, "in principle," from the motion of a meter needle, although there may be differences in the degree to which these various physical movements yield useful inferences.

The natural behaviorist, Petersen, will describe other people, and will observe them and think of them in terms of purely physical descriptions. We must assume that he can translate these into mental descriptions; otherwise he would be badly deficient in concepts. But he could, if he liked, refrain from making those translations. He could go for weeks on end, applying nothing but physical descriptions to other persons.

We might compare Petersen with someone who sees his physical environment as only two dimensional. He *knows* that it is three dimensional. He can infer the properties of bodies in the dimension of depth, from their properties (shape, size, color, motion) in the horizontal and vertical dimensions. He knows that a sailboat is moving away from or towards him; but he does not *see it as* receding, or as approaching. How could this fact come out? Perhaps one sign of it would be that he is never inclined to exclaim "See how fast that boat is coming towards us!" Also, he may be puzzled when others speak this

106. *Ibid.*, pp. 195–196.

way, and he may be ready to protest: "You *know* it is approaching but you don't *see* it approaching!"

Wittgenstein says the following of a triangle drawn in black lines on white paper:

> This triangle can be seen as a triangular hole, as a solid, as a geometrical drawing; as standing on its base, as hanging from its apex; as a mountain, as a wedge, as an arrow or pointer, as an overturned object which is meant to stand on the shorter side of the right-angle, as a half-parallelogram, and as various other things.[107]

We can imagine someone who is not able to see it in all of those ways. Perhaps he can see it as a figure on a flat surface, but not as a hole, or as a solid, or as horizontal, or as vertical. Or he may try to see it in each of these ways and succeed—or fail. Let us suppose he has to build a structure in accordance with an architect's drawing. One part of the drawing is a triangle. He cannot see it *as* a hole, although he knows that it represents a hole. He builds the structure accordingly.

This example provides an analogy for our conception of the natural behaviorist. The latter cannot see a human face *as* friendly or *as* angry. (Perhaps we should even say that he cannot see it *as a face*.) He does not see changes of expression *as such*. He sees the changes in a face only as physical alterations in three dimensions.

Wittgenstein makes this remark: "Think of the recognition of *facial expressions*. Or of the descrip-

107. Wittgenstein, *Investigations*, p. 200.

tion of facial expressions—which does not consist
in giving the measurements of the face! Think, too,
how one can imitate a man's face without seeing
one's own in a mirror.''[108]

We shall imagine that the form of description of a
face that comes most naturally to Petersen consists
in giving measurements. He sees faces and their expressions *under geometrical descriptions,* as we
might put it.

Similar things will be true in the auditory realm.
Petersen will hear human speech as changing in tone,
pitch, and volume, but not as *encouraging,* or as
*menacing,* or as *imploring.* Perhaps we should even
say that he will not hear the sounds produced by
people *as speech,* but will infer that it is speech. According to logical behaviorism the utterances, or
''speech movements,'' of a person are not in principle to be interpreted differently from the movements of a volt-meter. Petersen has enough general
information to know that when utterances with certain acoustical properties are emitted by a person in
certain circumstances, it can be inferred that the
person is asking a question, or replying to one, or stating something, and so on. But Petersen will not hear
someone's speech *as questioning,* or *as stating* something, or even *as saying* anything. He cannot be said
to lack information about people. Indeed, we are attributing to him a quite unusual amount of information, namely, sufficient theoretical knowledge to
enable him to make transitions, either inductively or

108. *Ibid.,* Sec. 285.

deductively, from purely physical descriptions to mental descriptions. (We do not have to believe that such knowledge is possible, but we shall suppose so for the purposes of this comparison.)

It is plain that Petersen differs greatly from us. Purely physical descriptions of human behavior do not come naturally to us. I am not even able to produce such descriptions. The case here is similar to the problem of how we perceive the physical world. Some philosophers have held that we do not *see* physical objects (bodies), or at least not *directly;* what we see directly are *colors* (color planes). But the truth is that if I were called upon to describe to you the room in which I am sitting, without employing the names of bodies ("chair," "lamp," "wall," "rug") but solely in terms of spatial relationships between color planes, I could not do it! This shows that it is false that what I *really see,* or *directly see,* are colors and not bodies. What those philosophers conceived to be the most basic form of description of *what we see* is actually a form of description that I (and people generally) cannot even employ. Perhaps with training and effort I could see my physical surroundings, when I go for a walk, not as trees, houses, and autos, but only as intersecting color planes. But to make the attempt now is to realize how remote this would be from my normal way of perceiving the physical world.

The same holds true of purely physical descriptions of human appearance and behavior. I can describe how someone looks by means of mental predicates ("angry," "sullen," "cheerful," "with-

drawn"). But I cannot give geometrical descriptions of facial expressions. Therefore it is false that
for me (and for people generally) the geometrical
description is the *basic* form of description, into
which and from which my mental descriptions of
facial expressions can be translated.

There is a parallel in the auditory realm. Sydney
Shoemaker says the following:

> We regard a person who is talking, not as making
> sounds from which, knowing the circumstances in
> which such sounds have been uttered in the past, we
> can make certain inductive inferences, but as *saying
> something*. We regard what he says as *having meaning*,
> not simply in the sense in which a barometer reading
> has meaning, i.e., as indicating that something has hap-
> pened, is happening, or is about to happen, but as ex-
> pressing what *he* means. It would be misleading to
> describe this as a *belief* on our part, the belief that
> people who use the words we use generally mean by
> them what we mean by them. It is rather a matter of
> attitude, of the way in which we respond to a person
> who is talking. . . . If this attitude were one of belief,
> we could inquire into the grounds of the belief. But
> this is just what we do not do. It is part of the expres-
> sion of this attitude that the question of what justifies
> us in regarding what others say as testimony does not
> arise. We say "I heard him say that he will come,"
> not "I heard him utter the sounds 'I will come,' and
> gathered from this that he was saying that he would
> come."[109]

Rarely do we perceive peoples' action in purely
physical terms. We perceive someone's speech as

109. Sydney Shoemaker, *Self-Knowledge and Self-Identity* (Ithaca,
N.Y., 1963), pp. 249–250.

passionate, and his movements as threatening. We perceive people under mental descriptions (as impatient, sad, affectionate) and we respond accordingly. This form of perception is natural for us, but not perception under a purely physical description. Perhaps we do not understand *how* this can be so; but this should not prevent us from recognizing that it *is* so.

Logical behaviorism holds that mental descriptions are equivalent to ("translatable" into) purely physical descriptions. This doctrine cannot be correct if the application to human beings of descriptions of the latter sort is something we do not even know how to manage. An equivalence of descriptions must require an equivalence *in use*.

Logical behaviorism is no longer as fashionable as it was in the 1930's. But a doctrine may lose its appeal for the wrong reasons. It is now widely acknowledged that it is impossible to provide, in complete detail, translations of mental descriptions into purely physical descriptions. Some philosophers may think that this is because the use of mental descriptions in ordinary language is vague and imprecise—neither exactly this nor exactly that. They may think that insofar as ordinary mental descriptions *have* any definite meaning, this can be explained by an analysis in physical terms. They may believe that logical behaviorism is *roughly* true, although not exactly true (because nothing would be exactly true).

In fact, however, logical behaviorism is a radically false view. It is just as false, and in a similar way, as is the idea that our basic perception of the physical world is of colored planes. We do not perceive the people with whom we work and chat, under purely physical descriptions first of all, and then infer mental descriptions. We differ from Petersen in two ways:

First, our perception of people under mental descriptions is *immediate,* in the sense that these descriptions are not based on descriptions of some different kind. This is not to deny that my perception of someone as sullen, or as amused, depends on my knowledge of his circumstances. But the point is that, given this knowledge, I *see amusement in his face,* or *sullenness in his posture.* I am not compelled to infer these things from something else I see.

Second, for the most part we cannot give or even comprehend purely physical descriptions of human behavior. Suppose I have conveyed to someone an important piece of information, and you want to know what his response was. Suppose I give you a description of it in physical terms (geometrical and acoustical), avoiding all mental terms. (I am not permitted, of course, to say that he *looked pleased* or *sounded embarrassed.*) You would not understand my description—that is, you would not know what his *response* was! You could not derive from this description the information you wanted, anymore than you could learn how my room is furnished from a description of it solely in terms of color planes.

Wittgenstein remarks that we have difficulty in imagining that a stone could have sensations, but we have no trouble at all in ascribing sensations to a wriggling insect. And he adds that "a corpse seems to us quite inaccessible to pain.—Our attitude to the living is not the same as to the dead. All our reactions are different.''[110]

Suppose that this difference in reactions did not come naturally to someone. We could not say that he was *wrong,* if his knowledge was as great, or greater, than ours. But he would be different. He would not have the concepts of pain, of consciousness, or of any mental predicates, *in the same way* we do. I am also inclined to say that he does not have the concept of a *person,* or at least not the same one we have.

Our reactions, our natural attitudes, towards the expressions, movements, and utterances of people constitute a dimension of our mental concepts. *This dimension is contributed by the perceiving, responding subject.*

Of the two criticisms of logical behaviorism we have put forward, one pertains to the ascription of mental predicates to oneself by oneself, the other to one's ascription of mental predicates to other people. The first criticism made a point that is by now pretty familiar to contemporary philosophers, namely, that a man's statements about his own intentions, thoughts and feelings, are not (by and large) based on his observation of his own behavior. Thus behaviorism's conception of the "content" of psychological sentences in the first person singular present tense indicative is erroneous.

110. Wittgenstein, *Investigations,* Sec. 284.

The second criticism is less familiar and is perhaps more difficult to grasp. It is an objection to behaviorism's account of the "content" of second and third person psychological sentences (singular and plural). On the behaviorist view, these sentences are translatable into sentences containing purely physical descriptions, and this form of description is conceived to be more fundamental than mental forms of description. We undertook to imagine a natural behaviorist—someone who perceived other people under purely physical descriptions and who *derived* the appropriate mental descriptions. The natural behaviorist would not perceive people *as frightened* or *as suffering,* although he would know that they were frightened or suffering. The mental concepts would not be embodied in his perception of people. It is clear that if he could not *see* a face as startled or as fearful, then his reactions to facial expressions could not be the same as ours. Since his natural attitudes conform to the theoretical viewpoint of logical behaviorism, the strangeness of his departure from what is normal shows that behaviorism does not give a true account of the way mental concepts are actually employed. And the behaviorist conception that purely physical descriptions are the more fundamental is completely wrong, since we cannot even apply this form of description to people. Thus behaviorism has a false understanding of mental terms, both as we apply them to ourselves and as we apply them to others.

73 74    12 11 10 9 8 7 6 5 4 3

Revised January, 1970

# hARPER ⚜ τORChBOOKS

## American Studies: General

HENRY ADAMS Degradation of the Democratic Dogma. ‡ Introduction by Charles Hirschfeld. TB/1450
LOUIS D. BRANDEIS: Other People's Money, and How the Bankers Use It. Ed. with Intro, by Richard M. Abrams TB/3081
HENRY STEELE COMMAGER, Ed.: The Struggle for Racial Equality TB/1300
CARL N. DEGLER: Out of Our Past: The Forces that Shaped Modern America CN/2
CARL N. DEGLER, Ed.: Pivotal Interpretations of American History
Vol. I TB/1240; Vol. II TB/1241
A. S. EISENSTADT, Ed.: The Craft of American History: Selected Essays
Vol. I TB/1255; Vol. II TB/1256
LAWRENCE H. FUCHS, Ed.: American Ethnic Politics TB/1368
MARCUS LEE HANSEN: The Atlantic Migration: 1607-1860. Edited by Arthur M. Schlesinger. Introduction by Oscar Handlin TB/1052
MARCUS LEE HANSEN: The Immigrant in American History. Edited with a Foreword by Arthur M. Schlesinger TB/1120
ROBERT L. HEILBRONER: The Limits of American Capitalism TB/1305·
JOHN HIGHAM, Ed.: The Reconstruction of American History TB/1068
ROBERT H. JACKSON: The Supreme Court in the American System of Government TB/1106
JOHN F. KENNEDY: A Nation of Immigrants. Illus. Revised and Enlarged. Introduction by Robert F. Kennedy TB/1118
LEONARD W. LEVY, Ed.: American Constitutional Law: Historical Essays TB/1285
LEONARD W. LEVY, Ed.: Judicial Review and the Supreme Court TB/1296
LEONARD W. LEVY: The Law of the Commonwealth and Chief Justice Shaw: The Evolution of American Law, 1830-1860 TB/1309
GORDON K. LEWIS: Puerto Rico: Freedom and Power in the Caribbean. Abridged edition TB/1371
GUNNAR MYRDAL: An American Dilemma: The Negro Problem and Modern Democracy. Introduction by the Author.
Vol. I TB/1443; Vol. II TB/1444
GILBERT OSOFSKY, Ed.: The Burden of Race: A Documentary History of Negro-White Relations in America TB/1405

ARNOLD ROSE: The Negro in America: The Condensed Version of Gunnar Myrdal's An American Dilemma. Second Edition TB/3048
JOHN E. SMITH: Themes in American Philosophy: Purpose, Experience and Community TB/1466
WILLIAM R. TAYLOR: Cavalier and Yankee: The Old South and American National Character TB/1474

## American Studies: Colonial

BERNARD BAILYN: The New England Merchants in the Seventeenth Century TB/1149
ROBERT E. BROWN: Middle-Class Democracy and Revolution in Massachusetts, 1691-1780. New Introduction by Author TB/1413
JOSEPH CHARLES: The Origins of the American Party System TB/1049
WESLEY FRANK CRAVEN: The Colonies in Transition: 1660-1712† TB/3084
CHARLES GIBSON: Spain in America † TB/3077
CHARLES GIBSON, Ed.: The Spanish Tradition in America + HR/1351
LAWRENCE HENRY GIPSON: The Coming of the Revolution: 1763-1775. † Illus. TB/3007
JACK P. GREENE, Ed.: Great Britain and the American Colonies: 1606-1763. + Introduction by the Author HR/1477
AUBREY C. LAND, Ed.: Bases of the Plantation Society + HR/1429
PERRY MILLER: Errand Into the Wilderness TB/1139
PERRY MILLER & T. H. JOHNSON, Ed.: The Puritans: A Sourcebook of Their Writings
Vol. I TB/1093; Vol. II TB/1094
EDMUND S. MORGAN: The Puritan Family: Religion and Domestic Relations in Seventeenth Century New England TB/1227
WALLACE NOTESTEIN: The English People on the Eve of Colonization: 1603-1630. † Illus. TB/3006
LOUIS B. WRIGHT: The Cultural Life of the American Colonies: 1607-1763. † Illus. TB/3005
YVES F. ZOLTVANY, Ed.: The French Tradition in America + HR/1425

## American Studies: The Revolution to 1860

JOHN R. ALDEN: The American Revolution: 1775-1783. † Illus. TB/3011

† The New American Nation Series, edited by Henry Steele Commager and Richard B. Morris.
‡ American Perspectives series, edited by Bernard Wishy and William E. Leuchtenburg.
a History of Europe series, edited by J. H. Plumb.
§ The Library of Religion and Culture, edited by Benjamin Nelson.
‖ Researches in the Social, Cultural, and Behavioral Sciences, edited by Benjamin Nelson.
Σ Harper Modern Science Series, edited by James A. Newman.
° Not for sale in Canada.
+ Documentary History of the United States series, edited by Richard B. Morris.
# Documentary History of Western Civilization series, edited by Eugene C. Black and Leonard W. Levy.
Λ The Economic History of the United States series, edited by Henry David et al.
¶ European Perspectives series, edited by Eugene C. Black.
** Contemporary Essays series, edited by Leonard W. Levy.
* The Stratum Series, edited by John Hale.

RAY A. BILLINGTON: The Far Western Frontier: 1830-1860. † *Illus.*　TB/3012

STUART BRUCHEY: The Roots of American Economic Growth, 1607-1861: *An Essay in Social Causation. New Introduction by the Author.*　TB/1350

WHITNEY R. CROSS: The Burned-Over District: *The Social and Intellectual History of Enthusiastic Religion in Western New York, 1800-1850*　TB/1242

NOBLE E. CUNNINGHAM, JR., Ed.: The Early Republic, 1789-1828 +　HR/1394

GEORGE DANGERFIELD: The Awakening of American Nationalism, 1815-1828. † *Illus.* TB/3061

CLEMENT EATON: The Freedom-of-Thought Struggle in the Old South. *Revised and Enlarged. Illus.*　TB/1150

CLEMENT EATON: The Growth of Southern Civilization, 1790-1860. † *Illus.*　TB/3040

ROBERT H. FERRELL, Ed.: Foundations of American Diplomacy, 1775-1872 +　HR/1393

LOUIS FILLER: The Crusade against Slavery: 1830-1860. † *Illus.*　TB/3029

DAVID H. FISCHER: The Revolution of American Conservatism: *The Federalist Party in the Era of Jeffersonian Democracy*　TB/1449

WILLIM W. FREEHLING: Prelude to Civil War: *The Nullification Controversy in South Carolina, 1816-1836*　TB/1359

PAUL W. GATES: The Farmer's Age: *Agriculture, 1815-1860* △　TB/1398

THOMAS JEFFERSON: Notes on the State of Virginia. ‡ *Edited by Thomas P. Abernethy*　TB/3052

FORREST MCDONALD, Ed.: Confederation and Constitution, 1781-1789 +　HR/1396

BERNARD MAYO: Myths and Men: *Patrick Henry, George Washington, Thomas Jefferson*　TB/1108

JOHN C. MILLER: Alexander Hamilton and the Growth of the New Nation　TB/3057

JOHN C. MILLER: The Federalist Era: 1789-1801. † *Illus.*　TB/3027

RICHARD B. MORRIS, Ed.: Alexander Hamilton and the Founding of the Nation. *New Introduction by the Editor*　TB/1448

RICHARD B. MORRIS: The American Revolution Reconsidered　TB/1363

CURTIS P. NETTELS: The Emergence of a National Economy, 1775-1815 △　TB/1438

DOUGLASS C. NORTH & ROBERT PAUL THOMAS, Eds.: *The Growth of the American Economy to 1860* +　HR/1352

R. B. NYE: The Cultural Life of the New Nation: 1776-1830. † *Illus.*　TB/3026

GILBERT OSOFSKY, Ed.: Puttin' On Ole Massa: *The Slave Narratives of Henry Bibb, William Wells Brown, and Solomon Northup* ‡　TB/1432

JAMES PARTON: The Presidency of Andrew Jackson. *From Volume III of the* Life of Andrew Jackson. *Ed. with Intro. by Robert V. Remini*　TB/3080

FRANCIS S. PHILBRICK: The Rise of the West, 1754-1830. † *Illus.*　TB/3067

MARSHALL SMELSER: The Democratic Republic, 1801-1815 †　TB/1406

JACK M. SOSIN, Ed.: The Opening of the West +　HR/1424

GEORGE ROGERS TAYLOR: The Transportation Revolution, 1815-1860 △　TB/1347

A. F. TYLER: Freedom's Ferment: *Phases of American Social History from the Revolution to the Outbreak of the Civil War. Illus.*　TB/1074

GLYNDON G. VAN DEUSEN: The Jacksonian Era: 1828-1848. † *Illus.*　TB/3028

LOUIS B. WRIGHT: Culture on the Moving Frontier　TB/1053

## American Studies: The Civil War to 1900

W. R. BROCK: An American Crisis: *Congress and Reconstruction, 1865-67* °　TB/1283

T. C. COCHRAN & WILLIAM MILLER: The Age of Enterprise: *A Social History of Industrial America*　TB/1054

W. A. DUNNING: Reconstruction, Political and Economic: 1865-1877　TB/1073

HAROLD U. FAULKNER: Politics, Reform and Expansion: 1890-1900. † *Illus.*　TB/3020

GEORGE M. FREDRICKSON: The Inner Civil War: *Northern Intellectuals and the Crisis of the Union*　TB/1358

JOHN A. GARRATY: The New Commonwealth, 1877-1890 †　TB/1410

JOHN A. GARRATY, Ed.: The Transformation of American Society, 1870-1890 +　HR/1395

HELEN HUNT JACKSON: A Century of Dishonor: *The Early Crusade for Indian Reform.* † *Edited by Andrew F. Rolle*　TB/3063

WILLIAM G. MCLOUGHLIN, Ed.: The American Evangelicals, 1800-1900: An Anthology ‡　TB/1382

ARNOLD M. PAUL: Conservative Crisis and the Rule of Law: *Attitudes of Bar and Bench, 1887-1895. New Introduction by Author*　TB/1415

JAMES S. PIKE: The Prostrate State: *South Carolina under Negro Government.* ‡ *Intro. by Robert F. Durden*　TB/3085

WHITELAW REID: After the War: *A Tour of the Southern States, 1865-1866.* ‡ *Edited by C. Vann Woodward*　TB/3066

FRED A. SHANNON: The Farmer's Last Frontier: *Agriculture, 1860-1897*　TB/1348

VERNON LANE WHARTON: The Negro in Mississippi, 1865-1890　TB/1178

## American Studies: The Twentieth Century

RICHARD M. ABRAMS, Ed.: The Issues of the Populist and Progressive Eras, 1892-1912 +　HR/1428

RAY STANNARD BAKER: Following the Color Line: *American Negro Citizenship in Progressive Era.* ‡ *Edited by Dewey W. Grantham, Jr. Illus.*　TB/3053

RANDOLPH S. BOURNE: War and the Intellectuals: *Collected Essays, 1915-1919.* ‡ *Edited by Carl Resek*　TB/3043

A. RUSSELL BUCHANAN: The United States and World War II. † *Illus.*
　　Vol. I TB/3044;　Vol. II TB/3045

THOMAS C. COCHRAN: The American Business System: *A Historical Perspective, 1900-1955*　TB/1080

FOSTER RHEA DULLES: America's Rise to World Power: 1898-1954. † *Illus.*　TB/3021

JEAN-BAPTISTE DUROSELLE: From Wilson to Roosevelt: *Foreign Policy of the United States, 1913-1945. Trans. by Nancy Lyman Roelker*　TB/1370

HAROLD U. FAULKNER: The Decline of Laissez Faire, 1897-1917　TB/1397

JOHN D. HICKS: Republican Ascendancy: 1921-1933. † *Illus.*　TB/3041

WILLIAM E. LEUCHTENBURG: Franklin D. Roosevelt and the New Deal: 1932-1940. † *Illus.*　TB/3025

WILLIAM E. LEUCHTENBURG, Ed.: The New Deal: *A Documentary History* +　HR/1354

ARTHUR S. LINK: Woodrow Wilson and the Progressive Era: 1910-1917. † *Illus.* TB/3023

BROADUS MITCHELL: Depression Decade: *From New Era through New Deal, 1929-1941* △  TB/1439

GEORGE E. MOWRY: The Era of Theodore Roosevelt and the Birth of Modern America: 1900-1912. † *Illus.*  TB/3022

WILLIAM PRESTON, JR.: Aliens and Dissenters: *Federal Suppression of Radicals, 1903-1933*  TB/1287

WALTER RAUSCHENBUSCH: Christianity and the Social Crisis. ‡ *Edited by Robert D. Cross*  TB/3059

GEORGE SOULE: Prosperity Decade: *From War to Depression, 1917-1929* △  TB/1349

GEORGE B. TINDALL, Ed.: A Populist Reader: *Selections from the Works of American Populist Leaders*  TB/3069

TWELVE SOUTHERNERS: I'll Take My Stand: *The South and the Agrarian Tradition. Intro. by Louis D. Rubin, Jr.; Biographical Essays by Virginia Rock*  TB/1072

## Art, Art History, Aesthetics

CREIGHTON GILBERT, Ed.: Renaissance Art **
*Illus.*  TB/1465

EMILE MALE: The Gothic Image: *Religious Art in France of the Thirteenth Century*. § *190 illus.*  TB/344

MILLARD MEISS: Painting in Florence and Siena After the Black Death: *The Arts, Religion and Society in the Mid-Fourteenth Century. 169 illus.*  TB/1148

ERWIN PANOFSKY: Renaissance and Renascences in Western Art. *Illus.*  TB/1447

ERWIN PANOFSKY: Studies in Iconology: *Humanistic Themes in the Art of the Renaissance. 180 illus.*  TB/1077

OTTO VON SIMSON: The Gothic Cathedral: *Origins of Gothic Architecture and the Medieval Concept of Order. 58 illus.*  TB/2018

HEINRICH ZIMMER: Myths and Symbols in Indian Art and Civilization. *70 illus.*  TB/2005

## Asian Studies

WOLFGANG FRANKE: China and the West: *The Cultural Encounter, 13th to 20th Centuries. Trans. by R. A. Wilson*  TB/1326

L. CARRINGTON GOODRICH: A Short History of the Chinese People. *Illus.*  TB/3015

DAN N. JACOBS, Ed.: The New Communist Manifesto and Related Documents.  TB/1078

DAN N. JACOBS & HANS H. BAERWALD, Eds.: Chinese Communism: *Selected Documents*  TB/3031

BENJAMIN I. SCHWARTZ: Chinese Communism and the Rise of Mao  TB/1308

BENJAMIN I. SCHWARTZ: In Search of Wealth and Power: *Yen Fu and the West*  TB/1422

## Economics & Economic History

C. E. BLACK: The Dynamics of Modernization: *A Study in Comparative History*  TB/1321

STUART BRUCHEY: The Roots of American Economic Growth, 1607-1861: *An Essay in Social Causation. New Introduction by the Author.*  TB/1350

GILBERT BURCK & EDITORS OF *Fortune*: The Computer Age: *And its Potential for Management*  TB/1179

SHEPARD B. CLOUGH, THOMAS MOODIE & CAROL MOODIE, Eds.: Economic History of Europe: *Twentieth Century* #  HR/1388

THOMAS C. COCHRAN: The American Business System: *A Historical Perspective, 1900-1955*  TB/1080

ROBERT A. DAHL & CHARLES E. LINDBLOM: Politics, Economics, and Welfare: *Planning and Politico-Economic Systems Resolved into Basic Social Processes*  TB/3037

PETER F. DRUCKER: The New Society: *The Anatomy of Industrial Order*  TB/1082

HAROLD U. FAULKNER: The Decline of Laissez Faire, 1897-1917 △  TB/1397

PAUL W. GATES: The Farmer's Age: *Agriculture, 1815-1860* △  TB/1398

WILLIAM GREENLEAF, Ed.: American Economic Development Since 1860 +  HR/1353

ROBERT L. HEILBRONER: The Future as History: *The Historic Currents of Our Time and the Direction in Which They Are Taking America*  TB/1386

ROBERT L. HEILBRONER: The Great Ascent: *The Struggle for Economic Development in Our Time*  TB/3030

DAVID S. LANDES: Bankers and Pashas: *International Finance and Economic Imperialism in Egypt. New Preface by the Author*  TB/1412

ROBERT LATOUCHE: The Birth of Western Economy: *Economic Aspects of the Dark Ages*  TB/1290

W. ARTHUR LEWIS: The Principles of Economic Planning. *New Introduction by the Author°*  TB/1436

WILLIAM MILLER, Ed.: Men in Business: *Essays on the Historical Role of the Entrepreneur*  TB/1081

GUNNAR MYRDAL: An International Economy. *New Introduction by the Author*  TB/1445

HERBERT A. SIMON: The Shape of Automation: *For Men and Management*  TB/1245

RICHARD S. WECKSTEIN, Ed.: Expansion of World Trade and the Growth of National Economies **  TB/1373

## Historiography and History of Ideas

J. BRONOWSKI & BRUCE MAZLISH: The Western Intellectual Tradition: *From Leonardo to Hegel*  TB/3001

WILHELM DILTHEY: Pattern and Meaning in History: *Thoughts on History and Society.° Edited with an Intro. by H. P. Rickman*  TB/1075

J. H. HEXTER: More's Utopia: *The Biography of an Idea. Epilogue by the Author*  TB/1195

H. STUART HUGHES: History as Art and as Science: *Twin Vistas on the Past*  TB/1207

ARTHUR O. LOVEJOY: The Great Chain of Being: *A Study of the History of an Idea*  TB/1009

RICHARD H. POPKIN: The History of Scepticism from Erasmus to Descartes. *Revised Edition*  TB/1391

MASSIMO SALVADORI, Ed.: Modern Socialism #  HR/1374

BRUNO SNELL: The Discovery of the Mind: *The Greek Origins of European Thought*  TB/1018

W. WARREN WAGER, ed.: European Intellectual History Since Darwin and Marx  TB/1297

## History: General

HANS KOHN: The Age of Nationalism: *The First Era of Global History*  TB/1380

BERNARD LEWIS: The Arabs in History  TB/1029

BERNARD LEWIS: The Middle East and the West °  TB/1274

## History: Ancient

A. ANDREWS: The Greek Tyrants  TB/1103

3

ERNST LUDWIG EHRLICH: A Concise History of Israel: *From the Earliest Times to the Destruction of the Temple in A.D. 70* ° TB/128
THEODOR H. GASTER: Thespis: *Ritual Myth and Drama in the Ancient Near East* TB/1281
MICHAEL GRANT: Ancient History ° TB/1190
A. H. M. JONES, Ed.: A History of Rome through the Fifth Century # *Vol. I: The Republic* HR/1364
*Vol. II The Empire:* HR/1460
NAPHTALI LEWIS & MEYER REINHOLD, Eds.: Roman Civilization *Vol. I: The Republic* TB/1231
*Vol. II: The Empire* TB/1232

## History: Medieval

MARSHALL W. BALDWIN, Ed.: Christianity Through the 13th Century # HR/1468
MARC BLOCH: Land and Work in Medieval Europe. *Translated by J. E. Anderson* TB/1452
HELEN CAM: England Before Elizabeth TB/1026
NORMAN COHN: The Pursuit of the Millennium: *Revolutionary Messianism in Medieval and Reformation Europe* TB/1037
G. G. COULTON: Medieval Village, Manor, and Monastery HR/1022
HEINRICH FICHTENAU: The Carolingian Empire: *The Age of Charlemagne. Translated with an Introduction by Peter Munz* TB/1142
GALBERT OF BRUGES: The Murder of Charles the Good: *A Contemporary Record of Revolutionary Change in 12th Century Flanders. Translated with an Introduction by James Bruce Ross* TB/1311
F. L. GANSHOF: Feudalism TB/1058
F. L. GANSHOF: The Middle Ages: *A History of International Relations. Translated by Rémy Hall* TB/1411
DENYS HAY: The Medieval Centuries ° TB/1192
DAVID HERLIHY, Ed.: Medieval Culture and Society # HR/1340
J. M. HUSSEY: The Byzantine World TB/1057
ROBERT LATOUCHE: The Birth of Western Economy: *Economic Aspects of the Dark Ages* ° TB/1290
HENRY CHARLES LEA: The Inquisition of the Middle Ages. || *Introduction by Walter Ullmann* TB/1456
FERDINARD LOT: The End of the Ancient World and the Beginnings of the Middle Ages. *Introduction by Glanville Downey* TB/1044
H. R. LOYN: The Norman Conquest TB/1457
ACHILLE LUCHAIRE: Social France at the time of Philip Augustus. *Intro. by John W. Baldwin* TB/1314
GUIBERT DE NOGENT: Self and Society in Medieval France: *The Memoirs of Guibert de Nogent.* || Edited by John F. Benton TB/1471
MARSILIUS OF PADUA: The Defender of Peace. *The Defensor Pacis. Translated with an Introduction by Alan Gewirth* TB/1310
CHARLES PETET-DUTAILLIS: The Feudal Monarchy in France and England: *From the Tenth to the Thirteenth Century* ° TB/1165
STEVEN RUNCIMAN: A History of the Crusades Vol. I: *The First Crusade and the Foundation of the Kingdom of Jerusalem. Illus.* TB/1143
Vol. II: *The Kingdom of Jerusalem and the Frankish East 1100-1187. Illus.* TB/1243
Vol. III: *The Kingdom of Acre and the Later Crusades. Illus.* TB/1298
J. M. WALLACE-HADRILL: The Barbarian West: *The Early Middle Ages, A.D. 400-1000* TB/1061

JACOB BURCKHARDT: The Civilization of the Renaissance in Italy. *Introduction by Benjamin Nelson and Charles Trinkaus. Illus.* Vol. I TB/40; Vol. II TB/41
JOHN CALVIN & JACOPO SADOLETO: A Reformation Debate. *Edited by John C. Olin* TB/1239
FEDERICO CHABOD: Machiavelli and the Renaissance TB/1193
J. H. ELLIOTT: Europe Divided, 1559-1598 *a* ° TB/1414
G. R. ELTON: Reformation Europe, 1517-1559 ° *a* TB/1270
DESIDERIUS ERASMUS: Christian Humanism and the Reformation: *Selected Writings. Edited and Translated by John C. Olin* TB/1166
DESIDERIUS ERASMUS: Erasmus and His Age: *Selected Letters. Edited with an Introduction by Hans J. Hillerbrand. Translated by Marcus A. Haworth* TB/1461
WALLACE K. FERGUSON et al.: Facets of the Renaissance TB/1098
WALLACE K. FERGUSON et al.: The Renaissance: *Six Essays. Illus.* TB/1084
FRANCESCO GUICCIARDINI: History of Florence. *Translated with an Introduction and Notes by Mario Domandi* TB/1470
WERNER L. GUNDERSHEIMER, Ed.: French Humanism, 1470-1600. * *Illus.* TB/1473
MARIE BOAS HALL, Ed.: Nature and Nature's Laws: *Documents of the Scientific Revolution* # HR/1420
HANS J. HILLERBRAND, Ed., The Protestant Reformation # TB/1342
JOHAN HUIZINGA: Erasmus and the Age of Reformation. *Illus.* TB/19
JOEL HURSTFIELD: The Elizabethan Nation TB/1312
JOEL HURSTFIELD, Ed.: The Reformation Crisis TB/1267
PAUL OSKAR KRISTELLER: Renaissance Thought: *The Classic, Scholastic, and Humanist Strains* TB/1048
PAUL OSKAR KRISTELLER: Renaissance Thought II: *Papers on Humanism and the Arts* TB/1163
PAUL O. KRISTELLER & PHILIP P. WIENER, Eds.: Renaissance Essays TB/1392
DAVID LITTLE: Religion, Order and Law: *A Study in Pre-Revolutionary England.* § *Preface by R. Bellah* TB/1418
NICCOLO MACHIAVELLI: History of Florence and of the Affairs of Italy: *From the Earliest Times to the Death of Lorenzo the Magnificent. Introduction by Felix Gilbert* TB/1027
ALFRED VON MARTIN: Sociology of the Renaissance. ° *Introduction by W. K. Ferguson* TB/1099
GARRETT MATTINGLY et al.: Renaissance Profiles. *Edited by J. H. Plumb* TB/1162
J. H. PARRY: The Establishment of the European Hegemony: 1415-1715: *Trade and Exploration in the Age of the Renaissance* TB/1045
J. H. PARRY, Ed.: The European Reconnaissance: *Selected Documents* # HR/1345
J. H. PLUMB: The Italian Renaissance: *A Concise Survey of Its History and Culture* TB/1161
A. F. POLLARD: Henry VIII. *Introductioh by A. G. Dickens.* ° TB/1249
RICHARD H. POPKIN: The History of Scepticism from Erasmus to Descartes TB/1391
PAOLO ROSSI: Philosophy, Technology, and the Arts, in the Early Modern Era 1400-1700. || *Edited by Benjamin Nelson. Translated by Salvator Attanasio* TB/1458

R. H. TAWNEY: The Agrarian Problem in the Sixteenth Century. *Intro. by Lawrence Stone* TB/1315

H. R. TREVOR-ROPER: The European Witch-craze of the Sixteenth and Seventeenth Centuries and Other Essays ° TB/1416

VESPASIANO: Rennaissance Princes, Popes, and XVth Century: *The Vespasiano Memoirs. Introduction by Myron P. Gilmore. Illus.* TB/1111

### History: Modern European

RENE ALBRECHT-CARRIE, Ed.: The Concert of Europe # HR/1341

MAX BELOFF: The Age of Absolutism, 1660-1815 TB/1062

OTTO VON BISMARCK: Reflections and Reminiscences. *Ed. with Intro. by Theodore S. Hamerow ¶* TB/1357

EUGENE C. BLACK, Ed.: British Politics in the Nineteenth Century # HR/1427

D. W. BROGAN: The Development of Modern France ° Vol. I: *From the Fall of the Empire to the Dreyfus Affair* TB/1184 Vol. II: *The Shadow of War, World War I, Between the Two Wars* TB/1185

ALAN BULLOCK: Hitler, A Study in Tyranny. ° *Revised Edition. Iuus.* TB/1123

GORDON A. CRAIG: From Bismarck to Adenauer: *Aspects of German Statecraft. Revised Edition* TB/1171

LESTER G. CROCKER, Ed.: The Age of Enlightenment # HR/1423

JACQUES DROZ: Europe between Revolutions, 1815-1848. ° *a Trans. by Robert Baldick* TB/1346

JOHANN GOTTLIEB FICHTE: Addresses to the German Nation. *Ed. with Intro. by George A. Kelly ¶* TB/1366

ROBERT & ELBORG FORSTER, Eds.: European Society in the Eighteenth Century # HR/1404

C. C. GILLISPIE: Genesis and Geology: *The Decades before Darwin §* TB/51

ALBERT GOODWIN: The French Revolution TB/1064

JOHN B. HALSTED, Ed.: Romanticism # HR/1387

STANLEY HOFFMANN et al.: In Search of France: *The Economy, Society and Political System In the Twentieth Century* TB/1219

H. STUART HUGHES: The Obstructed Path: *French Social Thought in the Years of Desperation* TB/1451

JOHAN HUIZINGA: Dutch Civilisation in the 17th Century and Other Essays TB/1453

WALTER LAQUEUR & GEORGE L. MOSSE, Eds.: Education and Social Structure in the 20th Century. ° *Volume 6 of the* Journal of Contemporary History TB/1339

WALTER LAQUEUR & GEORGE L. MOSSE, Ed.: International Fascism, 1920-1945. ° *Volume 1 of the* Journal of Contemporary History TB/1276

WALTER LAQUEUR & GEORGE L. MOSSE, Eds.: Literature and Politics in the 20th Century. ° *Volume 5 of the* Journal of Contemporary History. TB/1328

WALTER LAQUEUR & GEORGE L. MOSSE, Eds.: The New History: *Trends in Historical Research and Writing Since World War II.* ° *Volume 4 of the* Journal of Contemporary History TB/1327

WALTER LAQUEUR & GEORGE L. MOSSE, Eds.: 1914: *The Coming of the First World War.* ° *Volume3 of the* Journal of Contemporary History TB/1306

JOHN MCMANNERS: European History, 1789-1914: *Men, Machines and Freedom* TB/1419

PAUL MANTOUX: The Industrial Revolution in the Eighteenth Century: *An Outline of the Beginnings of the Modern Factory System in England* TB/1079

KINGSLEY MARTIN: French Liberal Thought in the Eighteenth Century: *A Study of Political Ideas from Bayle to Condorcet* TB/1114

NAPOLEON III: Napoleonic Ideas: *Des Idées Napoléoniennes, par le Prince Napoléon-Louis Bonaparte. Ed. by Brison D. Gooch ¶* TB/1336

FRANZ NEUMANN: Behemoth: *The Structure and Practice of National Socialism, 1933-1944* TB/1289

DAVID OGG: Europe of the Ancien Régime, 1715-1783 ° *a* TB/1271

GEORGE RUDE: Revolutionary Europe, 1783-1815 ° *a* TB/1272

MASSIMO SALVADORI, Ed.: Modern Socialism # TB/1374

DENIS MACK SMITH, Ed.: The Making of Italy, 1796-1870 # HR/1356

ALBERT SOREL: Europe Under the Old Regime, *Translated by Francis H. Herrick* TB/1121

ROLAND N. STROMBERG, Ed.: Realsim, Naturalism, and Symbolism: *Modes of Thought and Expression in Europe, 1848-1914* # HR/1355

A. J. P. TAYLOR: From Napoleon to Lenin: *Historical Essays* ° TB/1268

A. J. P. TAYLOR: The Habsburg Monarchy, 1809-1918: *A History of the Austrian Empire and Austria-Hungary* ° TB/1187

J. M. THOMPSON: European History, 1494-1789 TB/1431

DAVID THOMSON, Ed.: France: Empire and Republic, 1850-1940 # HR/1387

H. R. TREVOR-ROPER: Historical Essays ° TB/1269

W. WARREN WAGAR, Ed.: Science, Faith, and MAN: *European Thought Since 1914* # HR/1362

MACK WALKER, Ed.: Metternich's Europe, 1813-1848 # HR/1361

ELIZABETH WISKEMANN: Europe of the Dictators, 1919-1945 ° *a* TB/1273

JOHN B. WOLF: France: 1814-1919: *The Rise of a Liberal-Democratic Society* TB/3019

### Literature & Literary Criticism

JACQUES BARZUN: The House of Intellect TB/1051

W. J. BATE: From Classic to Romantic: *Premises of Taste in Eighteenth Century England* TB/1036

VAN WYCK BROOKS: Van Wyck Brooks: *The Early Years: A Selection from his Works, 1908-1921 Ed. with Intro. by Claire Sprague* TB/3082

RICHMOND LATTIMORE, Translator: The Odyssey of Homer TB/1389

ROBERT PREYER, Ed.: Victorian Literature ** TB/1302

BASIL WILEY: Nineteenth Century Studies: *Coleridge to Matthew Arnold* ° TB/1261

RAYMOND WILLIAMS: Culture and Society, 1780-1950 ° TB/1252

### Philosophy

HENRI BERGSON: Time and Free Will: *An Essay on the Immediate Data of Consciousness* ° TB/1021

LUDWIG BINSWANGER: Being-in-the-World: *Selected Papers. Trans. with Intro. by Jacob Needleman* TB/1365

H. J. BLACKHAM: Six Existentialist Thinkers: *Kierkegaard, Nietzsche, Jaspers, Marcel, Heidegger, Sartre* ° TB/1002

J. M. BOCHENSKI: The Methods of Contemporary Thought. *Trans. by Peter Caws* TB/1377
CRANE BRINTON: Nietzsche. *Preface, Bibliography, and Epilogue by the Author* TB/1197
ERNST CASSIRER: Rousseau, Kant and Goethe. *Intro. by Peter Gay* TB/1092
FREDERICK COPLESTON, S. J.: Medieval Philosophy TB/376
F. M. CORNFORD: From Religion to Philosophy: *A Study in the Origins of Western Speculation* § TB/20
WILFRID DESAN: The Tragic Finale: *An Essay on the Philosophy of Jean-Paul Sartre* TB/1030
MARVIN FARBER: The Aims of Phenomenology: *The Motives, Methods, and Impact of Husserl's Thought* TB/1291
PAUL FRIEDLANDER: Plato: *An Introduction* TB/2017
MICHAEL GELVEN: A Commentary on Heidegger's "Being and Time" TB/1464
J. GLENN GRAY: Hegel and Greek Thought TB/1409
W. K. C. GUTHRIE: The Greek Philosophers: *From Thales to Aristotle* ° TB/1008
G. W. F. HEGEL: On Art, Religion Philosophy: *Introductory Lectures to the Realm of Absolute Spirit.* || *Edited with an Introduction by J. Glenn Gray* TB/1463
G. W. F. HEGEL: Phenomenology of Mind. ° || *Introduction by George Lichtheim* TB/1303
MARTIN HEIDEGGER: Discourse on Thinking. *Translated with a Preface by John M. Anderson and E. Hans Freund. Introduction by John M. Anderson* TB/1459
F. H. HEINEMANN: Existentialism and the Modern Predicament TB/28
WERER HEISENBERG: Physics and Philosophy: *The Revolution in Modern Science. Intro. by F. S. C. Nortrop* TB/549
EDMUND HUSSERL: Phenomenology and the Crisis of Philosophy. § *Translated with an Introduction by Quentin Lauer* TB/1170
IMMANUEL KANT: Groundwork of the Metaphysic of Morals. *Translated and Analyzed by H. J. Paton* TB/1159
IMMANUEL KANT: Lectures on Ethics. § *Introduction by Lewis White Beck* TB/105
QUENTIN LAUER: Phenomenology: *Its Genesis and Prospect. Preface by Aron Gurwitsch* TB/1169
GEORGE A. MORGAN: What Nietzsche Means TB/1198
H. J. PATON: The Categorical Imperative: *A Study in Kant's Moral Philosophy* TB/1325
MICHAEL POLANYI: Personal Knowledge: *Towards a Post-Critical Philosophy* TB/1158
KARL R. POPPER: Conjectures and Refutations: *The Growth of Scientific Knowledge* TB/1376
WILLARD VAN ORMAN QUINE: Elementary Logic Revised Edition TB/577
MORTON WHITE: Foundations of Historical Knowledge TB/1440
WILHELM WINDELBAND: A History of Philosophy *Vol. I: Greek, Roman, Medieval* TB/38
*Vol. II: Renaissance, Enlightenment, Modern* TB/39
LUDWIG WITTGENSTEIN: The Blue and Brown Books ° TB/1211
LUDWIG WITTGENSTEIN: Notebooks, 1914-1916 TB/1441

## Political Science & Government

C. E. BLACK: The Dynamics of Modernization: *A Study in Comparative History* TB/1321
KENNETH E. BOULDING: Conflict and Defense: *A General Theory of Action* TB/3024

DENIS W. BROGAN: Politics in America. *New Introduction by the Author* TB/1469
ROBERT CONQUEST: Power and Policy in the USSR: *The Study of Soviet Dynastics* ° TB/1307
ROBERT A. DAHL & CHARLES E. LINDBLOM: Politics, Economics, and Welfare: *Planning and Politico-Economic Systems Resolved into Basic Social Processes* TB/1277
HANS KOHN: Political Ideologies of the 20th Century TB/1277
ROY C. MACRIDIS, Ed.: Political Parties: *Contemporary Trends and Ideas* ** TB/1322
ROBERT GREEN MC CLOSKEY: American Conservatism in the Age of Enterprise, 1865-1910 TB/1137
BARRINGTON MOORE, JR.: Political Power and Social Theory: *Seven Studies* || TB/1221
BARRINGTON MOORE, JR.: Soviet Politics—The Dilemma of Power: *The Role of Ideas in Social Change* || TB/1222
BARRINGTON MOORE, JR.: Terror and Progress—USSR: *Some Sources of Change and Stability in the Soviet Dictatorship* TB/1266
JOHN B. MORRALL: Political Thought in Medieval Times TB/1076
KARL R. POPPER: The Open Society and Its Enemies *Vol. I: The Spell of Plato* TB/1101
*Vol. II: The High Tide of Prophecy: Hegel, Marx, and the Aftermath* TB/1102
HENRI DE SAINT-SIMON: Social Organization, The Science of Man, and Other Writings. || *Edited and Translated with an Introduction by Felix Markham* TB/1152
JOSEPH A. SCHUMPETER: Capitalism, Socialism and Democracy TB/3008

## Psychology

LUDWIG BINSWANGER: Being-in-the-world: *Selected papers.* || *Trans. with Intro. by Jacob Needleman* TB/1365
HADLEY CANTRIL: The Invasion from Mars: *A Study in the Psychology of Panic* || TB/1282
MIRCEA ELIADE: Cosmos and History: *The Myth of the Eternal Return* § TB/2050
MIRCEA ELIADE: Myth and Reality TB/1369
MIRCEA ELIADE: Myths, Dreams and Mysteries: *The Encounter Between Contemporary Faiths and Archaic Realities* § TB/1320
MIRCEA ELIADE: Rites and Symbols of Initiation: *The Mysteries of Birth and Rebirth* § TB/1236
HERBERT FINGARETTE: The Self in Transformation: *Psychoanalysis, Philosophy and the Life of the Spirit* || TB/1177
SIGMUND FREUD: On Creativity and the Unconscious: *Papers on the Psychology of Art; Literature, Love, Religion.* § *Intro. by Benjamin Nelson* TB/45
J. GLENN GRAY: The Warriors: *Reflections on Men in Battle. Introduction by Hannah Arendt* TB/1294
WILLIAM JAMES: Psychology: *The Briefer Course. Edited with an Intro. by Gordon Allport* TB/1034
MUZAFER SHERIF: The Psychology of Social Norms. *Introduction by Gardner Murphy* TB/3072
HELLMUT WILHELM: Change: *Eight Lectures on the* I *Ching* TB/2019

## Religion: Ancient and Classical, Biblical and Judaic Traditions

C. K. BARRETT, Ed.: The New Testament Background: *Selected Documents* TB/86

7

MARTIN HEIDEGGER: Discourse on Thinking. *Translated with a Preface by John M. Anderson and E. Hans Freund. Introduction by John M. Anderson* TB/1459

IMMANUEL KANT: Religion Within the Limits of Reason Alone. § *Introduction by Theodore M. Greene and John Silber* TB/FG

H. RICHARD NIERUHR: Christ and Culture TB/3

H. RICHARD NIEBUHR: The Kingdom of God in America TB/49

JOHN H. RANDALL, JR.: The Meaning of Religion for Man. *Revised with New Intro. by the Author* TB/1379

*Science and Mathematics*

W. E. LE GROS CLARK: The Antecedents of Man: *An Introduction to the Evolution of the Primates.* ° *Illus.* TB/559

ROBERT E. COKER: Streams, Lakes, Ponds. *Illus.* TB/586

ROBERT E. COKER: This Great and Wide Sea: *An Introduction to Oceanography and Marine Biology. Illus.* TB/551

F. K. HARE: The Restless Atmosphere TB/560

WILLARD VAN ORMAN QUINE: Mathematical Logic TB/558

*Science: Philosophy*

J. M. BOCHENSKI: The Methods of Contemporary Thought. *Tr. by Peter Caws* TB/1377

J. BRONOWSKI: Science and Human Values. *Revised and Enlarged. Illus.* TB/505

WERNER HEISENBERG: Physics and Philosophy: *The Revolution in Modern Science. Introduction by F. S. C. Northrop* TB/549

KARL R. POPPER: Conjectures and Refutations: *The Growth of Scientific Knowledge* TB/1376

KARL R. POPPER: The Logic of Scientific Discovery TB/576

*Sociology and Anthropology*

REINHARD BENDIX: Work and Authority in Industry: *Ideologies of Management in the Course of Industrialization* TB/3035

BERNARD BERELSON, Ed., The Behavioral Sciences Today TB/1127

KENNETH B. CLARK: Dark Ghetto: *Dilemmas of Social Power. Foreword by Gunnar Myrdal* TB/1317

KENNETH CLARK & JEANNETTE HOPKINS: A Relevant War Against Poverty: *A Study of Community Action Programs and Observable Social Change* TB/1480

LEWIS COSER, Ed.: Political Sociology TB/1293

ROSE L. COSER, Ed.: Life Cycle and Achievement in America ** TB/1434

ALLISON DAVIS & JOHN DOLLARD: Children of Bondage: *The Personality Development of Negro Youth in the Urban South* || TB/3049

ST. CLAIR DRAKE & HORACE R. CAYTON: Black Metropolis: *A Study of Negro Life in a Northern City. Introduction by Everett C. Hughes. Tables, maps, charts, and graphs* Vol. I TB/1086; Vol. II TB/1087

PETER F. DRUCKER: The New Society: *The Anatomy of Industrial Order* TB/1082

LEON FESTINGER, HENRY W. RIECKEN, STANLEY SCHACHTER: When Prophecy Fails: *A Social and Psychological Study of a Modern Group that Predicted the Destruction of the World* || TB/1132

CHARLES Y. GLOCK & RODNEY STARK: Christian Beliefs and Anti-Semitism. *Introduction by the Authors* TB/1454

L. S. B. LEAKEY: Adam's Ancestors: *The Evolution of Man and His Culture. Illus.* TB/1019

KURT LEWIN: Field Theory in Social Science: *Selected Theoretical Papers.* || *Edited by Dorwin Cartwright* TB/1135

RITCHIE P. LOWRY: Who's Running This Town? *Community Leadership and Social Change* TB/1383

R. M. MACIVER: Social Causation TB/1153

GARY T. MARX: Protest and Prejudice: *A Study of Belief in the Black Community* TB/1435

ROBERT K. MERTON, LEONARD BROOM, LEONARD S. COTTRELL, JR., Editors: Sociology Today: *Problems and Prospects* ||
Vol. I TB/1173; Vol. II TB/1174

GILBERT OSOFSKY, Ed.: The Burden of Race: *A Documentary History of Negro-White Relations in America* TB/1405

GILBERT OSOFSKY: Harlem: The Making of a Ghetto: *Negro New York 1890-1930* TB/1381

TALCOTT PARSONS & EDWARD A. SHILS, Editors: Toward a General Theory of Action: *Theoretical Foundations for the Social Sciences* TB/1083

PHILIP RIEFF: The Triumph of the Therapeutic: *Uses of Faith After Freud* TB/1360

JOHN H. ROHRER & MUNRO S. EDMONSON, Eds.: The Eighth Generation Grows Up: *Cultures and Personalities of New Orleans Negroes* || TB/3050

ARNOLD ROSE: The Negro in America: *The Condensed Version of Gunnar Myrdal's* An American Dilemma. *Second Edition* TB/3048

GEORGE ROSEN: Madness in Society: *Chapters in the Historical Sociology of Mental Illness.* || *Preface by Benjamin Nelson* TB/1337

PHILIP SELZNICK: TVA and the Grass Roots: *A Study in the Sociology of Formal Organization* TB/1230

PITIRIM A. SOROKIN: Contemporary Sociological Theories: *Through the First Quarter of the Twentieth Century* TB/3046

MAURICE R. STEIN: The Eclipse of Community: *An Interpretation of American Studies* TB/1128

FERDINAND TONNIES: Community and Society: *Gemeinschaft und Gesellschaft. Translated and Edited by Charles P. Loomis* TB/1116

SAMUEL E. WALLACE: Skid Row as a Way of Life TB/1367

W. LLOYD WARNER and Associates: Democracy in Jonesville: *A Study in Quality and Inequality* || TB/1129

W. LLOYD WARNER: Social Class in America: *The Evaluation of Status* TB/1013

FLORIAN ZNANIECKI: The Social Role of the Man of Knowledge. *Introduction by Lewis A. Coser* TB/1372